CHRIST ABOVE ALL

By the same author

Islam: The House I Left Behind
Islam and the Son of God

For more information on Daniel Shayesteh's books

www.exodusfromdarkness.org

7spirits@gmail.com

CHRIST
ABOVE ALL

Conversational Evangelism
with People of Other Faiths

DANIEL SHAYESTEH

Talesh Books

Daniel Shayesteh, 1954–
Christ above all: conversational evangelism with people of other faiths
Published by Talesh Books, Sydney, Australia.
ISBN: 978-0-9756017-2-3

A previous version of this book was published as *Christ above all gods.*

Talesh Books are distributed in the USA and internationally by Ingram Book Group:
orders@ingrambook.com

Contents

PART III — THREE KEY QUESTIONS

PART IV — EVANGELISTIC CONVERSATIONS

PART V — CONCLUSION

Foreword

By Mark Durie

Conversation is at the heart of effective evangelism. Life-changing conversations are shaped by questions which have the capacity to open people's hearts and minds to new possibilities. A well-timed question has the capacity to crack open a worldview along its fault-lines, exposing inner inconsistencies, and helping someone to put their finger on the flaws in their own thinking. It can also suggest new ways of understanding, opening up new possibilities for looking at the world.

To ask the right question of another person, it is necessary to know your way around their belief system. If you do not know where the other person is coming from, and the implications of what they believe, your conversions with them could be like two ships passing each other in the night, without any genuine engagement.

An obstacle to meaningful conversations in today's multicultural, multifaith world, is that all around us people follow so many different belief systems. How can we learn about these widely different beliefs, and equip ourselves to conserve meaningfully with those who accept them? One of the difficulties is that the key controlling assumptions of belief systems can be hidden from view, difficult to identify, and may not be obvious, least of all to the person who adheres to them.

Christ Above All is a valuable resource for Christians who want to overcome these problems. In it Dr Daniel Shayesteh offers a practical road map for a wide variety of belief systems, from Communism to the New Age, and Zoroastrianism to Islam. Not only is each belief system summarized and its key weaknesses exposed, but Dr Shayesteh has formulated telling questions which can be brought forward in conversations with adherents of each set of beliefs. Until you are familiar with a particular belief system, the significance of each question may not be apparent, but if you understand a belief system, and are familiar with its weaknesses, the right question can be a powerful tool in your hand.

In these matters, Dr Shayesteh is no mere theoretician. Dr Shayesteh has put the principles contained in this book into practice on countless occasions over decades. His tools for conversational evangelism have enabled him to win many to faith in Christ, including many Muslims. *Christ Above All* is informed by a life-long interest in philosophy and comparative religions. An Iranian by birth, who comes from a multi-ethnic home on the edge of the Caspian sea, Dr Shayesteh's personal search for the meaning of life was a long one, leading him at different stages to communism, radical Islam and finally to a vibrant faith in Christ, the Son of God. He knows what it is to shed blood for one's convictions, and has lost friends to Iran's ideological purges. Moreover, years of living in the West as an 'outsider' and his unique life experiences have enabled him to dissect Western belief systems, including the New Age and Secular Humanism, with fresh and skeptical eyes.

One of the themes of *Christ Above All* is the pursuit of intellectual confidence. For Dr Shayesteh, confidence of mind must be grounded in a moral standard, which establishes a well-grounded ability to distinguish right from wrong. His criticism of Humanism, for example, is that anything and everything is good for the humanist, because humanistic ideology is ultimately grounded in random evolutionary processes: even the mind itself is reduced to mere matter. This moral failing of humanism is the key to understanding its inability to satisfy the human intellect.

The solution to failing world views, Dr Shayesteh argues, is to follow Jesus Christ: "The Gospel of Jesus Christ claims that peace and love come from a pure heart, a good conscience, and a sincere faith, which encourage understanding and affirm confidence." May this innovative book, packed with fresh ideas, be a powerful resource in the hands of all who wish to lead others to confidence in Christ.

Preface

This book focuses on three major areas:

1. The philosophical problems of other religions and philosophies which are resolved in Christianity. (e.g. the personal oneness of God in the Bible in contrast to the dualistic nature of other gods);

2. How to have an effective conversation with the adherents of non-Christian religions and philosophies;

3. Examples of actual dialogues with non-Christians.

The growth of technology is transforming the world into a global village. No country in the world is completely run by a homogenous cultural or religious group anymore. Even the most closed countries are faced with the pressures of this transformation.

For example, due to massive immigration, population decline and the weakness of the Christian faith, Europe is being transformed into an Islamic island, a process which is likely to be completed by the end of this century. What is worse, Christians in Europe are not prepared to meet this challenge. It is the conviction of this writer that western Christians (their beliefs and values) must convert these immigrants or be converted by them.

Patently, every belief system in the world counters the Christianity's worldview. This opposition is expressed in two ways: One is an overt opposition which is normally the case in countries that are led by communists or Islamists; The second is an indirect (sometimes direct) opposition in non-Islamic countries, mainly in the West, by Islamists, atheists, secular and cosmic humanists, and the agents of Eastern religions. Sadly, Christians are not prepared to answer this opposition. In the name of democracy, pluralism and multiculturalism, unwary Christians have left themselves vulnerable to the hostile non-Christian beliefs that are determined to uproot Christian faith and values. Christ expects His churches to be awake, to be alive and to give the light of the glorious gospel that leads people from captivity to freedom—freedom from tyranny and oppression (Ephesians 5:14). But today churches are ignorant of the ultimate intentions of their enemies—non-Christian religions and philosophies. In the name of "tolerance," they accommodate and harbor these enemies of liberty at the cost of their own freedoms and live-giving values.

It is the contention of this writer that the Christian faith is relevant to all of life and has every explanation for everything in all dimensions of life. On the other hand, non-Christian religions and philosophies have deep problems in their explanations of life and reality. If we can point out what these problems are and present a biblical answer, it is possible that many will be enlightened and perhaps

> *God will give them repentance to the acknowledging of the truth, and that they awake out of the snare of the Devil, having been taken captive by him, so as to do the will of that one.* (2 Timothy 2:25).

It is imperative that we understand the problems with non-Christian world-views and prepare ourselves to counter them with attractive and irrefutable reasoning from the Bible so that they can receive the message of Christ with their mind, heart and soul and in the understanding of it to rejoice in it.

The Gospel of Christ states that Jesus is the **Lord of lords, King of kings** (Revelation 19:16). This is true in every aspect of life. For this reason His message is meant for every nation, tribe, language and people (Revelation 7:9; 14:6). It is for all—for the religious and the non-religious alike. But it will not be accepted until we can prove its superiority to the beliefs and philosophies of non-Christians. To present this message to them then we need to know the fundamental problems with their beliefs so that we can open their eyes to the unique and saving message of Jesus Christ.

The Lord invites people to reason with Him. He says, "Come now let us reason together" (Isaiah 1:18). The Bible says, "…the Lord will give you understanding in all things" (2 Timothy 2:7). The Lord has given to all men the ability to reason. He gives to each Christian the responsibility of giving a defense to anyone who asks a reason for the hope we have in Christ (1 Peter 3:15). So in Christ, we can answer every question of life, but if we do not learn how to show them the superiority of Christ we will not be able to convince them of His truth and they will not be saved.

Also, reasoning with non-Christians requires that we build trusted relationships before we can present the truth of Christ to them. It is also important to remember that we can only demonstrate our genuine relationship with God if we have spent time with him in his word and in prayer. Then we will have his love for and his perspective of those with whom we speak. What a privilege! God has ordained that through biblical understanding and reasoning we can be winners of souls for His kingdom.

Non-Christians have the capacity to understand the truth and to decide whether they will believe it or not. For example, God has said that His law is written in the hearts of all men and that their consciences bear witness to the truth of it (Romans 2:14-16). Therefore, if we present the truth of God plainly and appeal to their consciences (2 Corinthians 4:2) then the law (values) of God will lead them to Christ (Galatians 3:24).

It should be stressed that our reasoning should be based on the Bible. The Bible is preeminent in giving understanding and in discovering the truth of God:

> *All Scripture is God-breathed, and is profitable for doctrine, for reproof, for correction, for instruction in righteousness, that the man of God may be perfected, thoroughly furnished to every good work.* (2 Timothy 3:16-17).

Biblical reasoning rejects passivity, fanaticism and violence; it establishes a basis for reconciliation among the nations and between the nations and God. It is only through biblical reasoning that anyone can understand the truth of God and experience the power of God in their lives:

> *For the Word of God is living and powerful and sharper than any two-edged sword ...* (Hebrew 4:12).

If non-believers could see the superiority of Christ in comparison to their own gods and the salutary effects of His message compared to their own beliefs (Acts 4:12), they will surely give their hearts to Him. For what man has ever **truly** tasted of the goodness of Christ and been able to turn away disappointed? None! "*Oh, taste and see that the LORD is good...*" (Psalm 34:8).

I pray that this book may become a blessed tool for many who have not had the opportunity to evaluate the deeper layers of their beliefs and who were not aware of how that their own individual life and the lives of their families and of their societies could be invaded by false gods and false beliefs.

I also take this opportunity to express my appreciation to all those who have encouraged me to write this book and who have helped to bring it to its present stage. However, they have not contributed in any way to formulating the arguments and conclusions I have made throughout the book; I take full responsibility for what is written.

Daniel Shayesteh

Introduction

PART I

1

The Importance of Beliefs

Why Do People Follow a Belief?

There are a variety of reasons why people follow one belief in preference to another.

Self-Preservation

Often it is not personal choice, but external forces which have imposed a particular belief or religion upon a people group,. For example, when people are unable to control surrounding human or natural forces, they may prefer to show allegiance rather than be killed. The same applies when people are compelled to follow a certain religion.

To Please "God"

Some, who believe in a "creator" of the universe, may revere him (or "it" in some religions) as the highest authority, and desire to be under his/its control and in harmony with him/it.

To Please the Community

Some follow the religion practiced by their community in order to have acceptance within their community.

For Self-Fulfillment

The development of civilization has led some to search for an explanation which offers purpose, goals and hope for their lives, and indeed for life itself. This can lead them to select an idea or religion which best meets their needs and assists them to attain their goals.

Why Understand People's Beliefs?

Beliefs Affect Behavior

Willingly or unwillingly, every person in the world is affected by their beliefs. Different ethnic groups hold values and beliefs which cause them to act and react in different ways from other people of other ethnic backgrounds, at least in some respects. There are differences everywhere, and these differences are reflected throughout society and in everyone's relationship with one another. Religious people are affected by non-religious people and visa versa. Even atheists, whose philosophy is against religion, have not been able to live without the influence of religious morals and principles. Their own ungodly philosophies have also influenced societies to an unbelievable extent. Religious values are present everywhere we go; they are present in the lives of everybody with whom we have contact. Therefore, understanding each other's beliefs is of vital importance for the well-being of a society. It helps us to discover long lasting values for establishing relationships and friendships with one another. Ignorance, indifference, and passive tolerance which comes from a lack of understanding—these enhance miscommunication and alienation and can create catastrophic events in the world, such as happened on September 11, which are heartbreaking and forever irreparable. There are countless examples of different communities who have lived in the same country side by side for centuries and in some cases even for thousands of years, but are still alien or hostile to each other. The main reason for this is misunderstanding.

The Impact of Globalization

Another influence we see today is the internationalization of technology (globalization), which has brought people of various nations together and forced almost all nations of the world to become multicultural—a blessing in many ways. However, a crisis arises where people do not understand each other and are not integrated peacefully.

Tolerant secularism (democracy) is not able to provide people with an adequate understanding of multiculturalism. It welcomes people from all cultural and religious backgrounds, but ignores the great need to understand the deeper cultural or religious beliefs carried by each person when they travel to new places. The fruit of secular democracy is a 'passive' tolerance, which means being unable or unwilling to question the validity of other people's beliefs. This is quite unlike the patient tolerance of God, which promotes knowledge and incites people to quest after what is best: this of course reflects what He thinks is best as revealed in His Word. Passive tolerance is not godlike perseverance: it is a willfully ignorant and carelessly indifferent tolerance, which can be as harmful as aggression because in the end it permits and even incites an aggressive defiance of God's laws for society.

Many believed that through the advancement of technology, together with sovereign social laws, the authorities would be able to create a more welcoming and friendly atmosphere which could help lead multi-ethnic societies towards integration and social cohesion. However they neglected the dynamic effect of religion, so they overlooked the fact that people can have more respect for their religious beliefs than for the laws of a society. Some religious people believe that, in some cases, they have to break society's laws for the sake of religious conviction. Clearly, religion has a deep root in people's ethical, moral, political, economic and social values, and it must be deeply understood.

People tend to only look at the external layers of beliefs and are disinterested in bringing the deeper layers to surface. Religious messages are said to be all the same and heading toward the same goal. Very few have looked at the deeper layers of religion and analyzed the fundamental nature of the various gods in order to see whether or not they are the same. That is why whenever religious conflicts arise between groups, many shake their heads and say, 'They are heading toward the same goal; why they are against each other?' Unfortunately very few have made a scholarly study of the differences between faiths. Time and time again we hear someone say, 'Well, it's the different interpretations of their religion which have led them to do this or that, or have led them to acts of terrorism'. While it is true that differences in interpretation can be a cause for conflict, all too often the problem lies in the fundamental characteristics of a religion. Blaming conflicts on 'interpretation' reveals ignorance and a lack of understanding of the deeper issues. In the world today such ignorance is itself a profound obstacle to human liberty.

Unfortunately, the average person is not interested in spending time evaluating the motivations which lie 'behind the scenes' of religions, and can have major effects over time. Moreover, leaders in various countries have realized this, and have exploited public indifference and ignorance. They can pretend to be for the people, and keepers of peace and justice, yet they only look after their own interests. Some have laced their dictatorship with religious and doctrinal values in order to ensnare ignorant people in the claws of their own selfish desires.

Nothing other than 'knowledge and understanding' can rescue people from theses threats. As the Bible states:

> *Because of the transgression of a land, many are its princes; but by a man of understanding and knowledge Right will be prolonged* (Proverb 28:2).

Religious and ideological problems cannot be solved through political pressure, or through the authority of social laws. This is because people's beliefs and ideas have a determining influence over all other aspects of life. The only way to resolve ideological problems is to aim at people's hearts, minds and consciences. People need encouragement and help to broaden their understanding and evaluate competing ideas, so they can choose what is true and genuine. However to undertake this process of evaluation is costly in some countries, even resulting in the death penalty for those who attempt it. On the other hand, those who do have freedom to evaluate the foundations of their faith and values can reach out to those who have been deprived of this freedom, and share what they have learned with them. This is the value of evangelism and missions work.

The Basis for Bringing about a Change in the Quality of People's Lives

Knowledge and information opens the eyes of people and enables them to improve the quality of their lives—physically and spiritually. Conversely, ignorance deprives people of this ability and drives them toward narrow-minded extremes, thus degrading the quality of their life. The quality of life improves when people are open-minded but it declines when they are closed-minded. A beautiful life cannot be attained by a passive mind. It would be a shame for the author of life to have blind followers. Look what the God of Israel said to her, even though she was honoring Him with the best of her wealth:

> *For the Lord has spoken: "I have nourished and brought up children, and they have rebelled against Me; The ox knows its owner and the donkey its master's crib; but Israel does not know, my people do not consider...I do not delight in the blood of bulls or of lambs or goats...Bring no more futile sacrifices. Incense is an abomination to Me...Come now, and let us reason together,* (Isaiah 1:2-3, 11c, 13a, 18a).

> *Who is blind but My servant, or deaf as My messenger whom I send? Who is blind as he who is perfect, And blind as the LORD's servant? Seeing many things, but you do not observe; opening the ears, but he does not hear." The LORD is well*

> *pleased for His righteousness sake; He will exalt the law and make it honorable* (Isaiah 42:19-21).

God had no pleasure in the people's sacrifices while they continued to close their eyes to deeper understanding. A belief must not be blindly accepted or rejected without careful consideration. We are the creatures of insight, reason and logic. Rejecting one idea and accepting another without an understanding of the basic tenets of either is like being blind and deaf. Can we bring glory to God through willful ignorance?

Research and investigation are beneficial in every situation. They will save the world from the crises of falsely grounded religions and ideas and lead it to unity and peace. Consider the Bible's counsel for openness, research and comparison in decision-making:

> *Does not the ear test words and the mouth taste its food?* (Job 12:11; 34:3)

> *Receive my instruction, and not silver, And knowledge rather than choice gold* (Proverb 8:10,14).

> *You will seek Me and find Me, when your search for Me with all your heart. I will be found by you, says the LORD, …* (Jeremiah 29: 13-14).

> *You shall know the truth, and the truth shall make you free* (John 8:32).

> *Test all things; hold fast what is good. Abstain from every form of evil* (1 Thessalonians 5:21-22).

> *If you say in your heart, 'How shall we know the word which the LORD has not spoken?' – when a prophet speaks in the name of the LORD, if the thing does not happen or come to pass, that is the thing which the LORD has not spoken; the prophet has spoken it presumptuously; you shall not be afraid of him* (Deuteronomy 18:21-22).

> *Beware lest anyone cheat you through philosophy and empty deceit, according to the tradition of men, according to the basic*

> *principles of the world, and not according to Christ* (Colossians 2:8).
>
> *Professing to be wise, they became fools, and changed the glory of the incorruptible God into an image made like corruptible man – and birds and four-footed animals and creeping things* (Romans 1:22-23).
>
> *That their hearts may be encouraged, being knit together in love, and attaining to all riches of the full assurance of understanding, to the knowledge of the mystery of God, both of the Father and of Christ* (Colossians 2:2).

No other religion in the world has encouraged such a deep understanding of what is needed to escape the evil consequences of willful ignorance and blind obedience.

Our contemporary world is seeking expand knowledge at a time when people should be seeking solid answers to the most difficult questions of life. In fact, the need to examine one's beliefs is more urgent today than since the beginning of time. This is because internationalization and globalization have blurred national borders, overridden natural barriers, and brought people much closer to one another. In this context, people need to examine the deeper cultural and religious values of the peoples of the earth, in order to discover the best values for a better integration of the world. The omnipresent and omniscient Spirit of Christ supports this process.

Jesus claimed that He was the Lord for all people for all time (Matthew 28:18-20; Hebrew 13:8). He certainly is pleased with those who have a global view of life in this world. Yet, He has also warned against a secular world view (Matthew 6:19-34; 7:15-29), which leads people astray from God's purpose and design for human life, a view that destroys human relationships and eventually the world itself, a view that attempts to impose itself forcefully on people living in God's world, a view that comes from the pit of hell. It is for this reason that people need to have intelligent reasons for everything they believe and for choosing who they will follow.

True and Genuine Belief

1. A true, genuine and credible belief system is able to establish truth in the hearts and lives of people in a practical way and distinguish it from evil.

2. It respects the free will of every individual in the world.

3. It does not impose itself on others, but respects the voice of free will and is open to criticism.

4. It does not act from ulterior motives, but encourages honesty as an essential quality of life-giving human relationships.

5. It seeks to serve humankind by becoming a tool for the development of understanding among diverse nations in order to remove the barriers to unity.

6. It allows people to scrutinize its values and its leader's life in order to fully understand the concepts and ideas which form the basis of that belief.

7. It calls upon people to search for the best possible values in the world and choose the best with a free will. The truth cannot be discovered by blindly following or obeying the guidance of someone who has never been open to comparison and has never allowed others to do it.

8. It overcomes any uncertainty and gives certainty for the future.

A true and genuine believe system meets the 'at all times' criterion of truthfulness, and provides a good example for all generations.

It is my hope that this book will become a fruitful tool in the hands of Christians for helping non-Christians to discover the Truth of Christ with open eyes.

2

Evangelism Engages People with Questions of Life

Right and Timely Questions

The right question, asked at the right time, can completely change the direction of someone's life. Life-changing conversations take place when:

- You understand the other person's worldview;
- You invite them into a process of discovery;
- You know which questions to ask;
- You can anticipate their responses and are ready with answers; and
- You can give solid and sensible reasons for your faith.

Why Do We Need to Invite People into a Process of Discovery?

God is the God of reason. He gives understanding in all things (2 Timothy 2:7) and challenges people to give reasons for their life (Isaiah 1:18). He sets forth reasons that build relationships with people. For this reason, we also need to be armed with reasons for our faith and be available to God to help us express to others those reasons in a clear and effective manner. Those who understand God's mind and heart will love Him with all their mind and heart (Matthew 22:37) and will be able to teach God's truth effectively (Matthew 28:20; Hebrew 4:12).

According to the Gospel of Christ, people have a capacity to understand the truth and to make intelligent decisions (John 8:32) when they are challenged to do so:

The law of God is written on the hearts of people and their consciences bear witness to it (Romans 2:14-16). So, there is a witness of God in the heart of every person in the world.

Therefore, if '*we set forth the truth of Christ plainly and commend ourselves to every person's conscience in the sight of God*' (2 Corinthians 4:2), a person's conscience will confirm the witness of God and they will be challenged to compare and decide. This is because the law (values) of God in the heart of every person is there to lead them to Christ (Galatians 3:24).

This is an amazing and fair advantage for Christian evangelism. If we are able to get people into conversation, and if they remain with the conversation till the end, and if we are able to challenge them, doubtless they will all give their hearts to Jesus. I have experienced this myself and for this reason was encouraged to reflect on my experiences and explain them in this book.

We need to engage people in conversation because:

- Reason rejects passivity, fanaticism and violence, and establishes reconciliation among individuals, nations, and between nations and God: violence in the family or among the nations of the world is not removed unless people are open to reason.
- People need to experience the power of the message of Christ personally (Hebrews 4:12).
- People need to compare the superiority of Christ with their own gods or ultimate realities (Revelation 17:14; 19:16), and the effectiveness of the message of Christ with their own beliefs and philosophies (Acts 4:12).

People Need to Be Encouraged that They Are Capable

In your conversations with others, always encourage them by saying that they are interested in the Truth and are capable of discovering it. Comments or questions such as following are encouraging:

- I am sure that you love the truth and have a reason for believing it.
- By the way, how is the truth best understood?
- Don't you think the truth will be better understood if we explore the definition for truth from the perspective of the world? In other words, wouldn't we need to know how others define the truth, and which definition is the best?
- Do you think everybody knows the truth? If not, don't we have a responsibility to help them know and understand it?
- Do you think that everybody should embrace the truth?
- Do you believe that people have the capacity to understand the truth?
- Don't you believe that people need to understand each other's beliefs, so that by communicating with one another they might discover the truth?

The Way You Guide the Conversation

Like the Bible, we need to challenge people's consciences. Taking people to the root of their beliefs is the best approach. A few considerations show the value of this approach:

1. "*If the root is holy, so are the branches*" (Romans 11:16c). If we are talking about the nature of God, we can say, 'If God is holy so are His followers. Likewise, if God is not holy, neither will be His followers.'

2. Can imperfection lead to perfection? (1 Corinthians 13:10) The answer is obviously 'No.' We must be able to prove from the Bible that since Allah is not perfect, he is unable to make his followers perfect. And if he is not perfect, then his book, the Quran, and his way, Islam, will not be perfect either.

3. Who can bring purity from impurity? To this vital question Job responds, "*No one but God*" (Job 14:4). All other religions believe that impure humanity can save itself. It is important that people see themselves as impure sinners who are unable to save themselves by their own self-righteousness works: "*We have all become like one who is unclean, and all our righteous deeds are like a polluted garment,*" (Isaiah 64:6). For salvation comes not by works but by the grace of God (Galatians 2:16; Ephesians 2:8-9; 2 Timothy 1:9; Titus 3:5).

4. Can someone teach freedom or be the messenger of freedom while he himself is not free? For example, Muhammad was not free from sin: how then can he bring freedom to others?

5. Can someone be a peace-maker without living in the Kingdom of Peace, or without submission to the source of absolute peace?

6. Can someone be a good, moral and ethical example without having God's moral principles written on his heart?

If someone is not in a perfect spiritual environment and is not living with a holy God, he will have no authority to speak of holiness, perfection or peace. Jesus Christ tells His disciples that He will send His Holy Spirit to dwell in them and teach them Truth (John 14:26-27). This declaration is for all who are born again. It is necessary to understand that *unless you are born again* you cannot be indwelled by God's Spirit and therefore will not be saved, nor will you be a credible witness about freedom, holiness, perfection, peace.

In order to challenge people, we need to follow the Bible's lead, encouraging them to use their God-given capability for discovering and discerning the truth.

The Significance of These Questions

The questions given at the end of this chapter can be used to start discussions about the root of a belief, so that people might be able to discover a reliable standard for life. Every individual needs an absolute standard which leads to freedom and peace, and which prevents them from trampling the rights of others. If people discover that their philosophy or their god is against freedom, unity and peace, they will be challenged and motivated to search for the truth. Eventually they will believe in Christ.

Faith in Christ Is Reasonable

We can be confident that there are clear and rational reasons for our faith in Christ and we make sure we are equipped to defend it against all other beliefs and religions. Post modernist ideas have so poisoned the minds of many, that they have become convinced that faith in Christ has nothing to do with intellectual rigor and reason. We need to challenge the followers of all beliefs and philosophies which have rejected reason and believe in the randomness of evolution or in dictatorship. They need to understand that intellectual honesty and integrity stands against all philosophies which make no distinction between right and wrong. For Post-modernists, everything is right; there is no way to evaluate their presuppositions. Consequently, if they claim there is no difference between right and wrong they are unable to deny God or to denounce the Christian position. In the same way, beliefs that deny human freedom do not come from the all-knowing God who has granted the gift of reason, which enables people to be convinced about the truth.

All other beliefs and philosophies rely on relativistic thinking; they cannot be proven true rationally. The Bible is the word of a reasonable God (Isaiah 1:18), and its message can be tested and proved true (1 Thessalonians 5:21). We Christians are better able than the followers of other beliefs to answer questions of life because our faith offers certainty to people's hearts and through reason is proved to be true and superior to other faiths or philosophies. This is a fair advantage which Christians enjoy. They are given a perfect heavenly identity in Christ (Colossians 2:10), and out of this perfection, Christians can find answers to the questions of life for themselves and for others more perfectly (1 Peter 3:15).

Now thanks be to God, who always leads us in triumph in Christ, and through us diffuses the fragrance of His knowledge in every place. (2 Corinthians 2:14).

A List of Questions of Life

Questions vary according to the nature of the conversation. Here is a list of questions to use in evangelistic conversations with others. They are presented in four groups:

1) Questions about philosophies;

2) Questions about religions;

3) Questions about God, Satan and creation;

4) Questions about sin and humanity.

Questions about Philosophies

Why do you (a humanist or atheist) reject the existence of supernatural beings (none matter, including God) while you claim that matter is created from non-matter?

How does life come from nothing?

How can you know the purpose of life, if there is no indication from the source of that life?

What is the purpose of your life, if you come from nothing, are nothing and go to nothing?

How do you distinguish good from bad and right from wrong, if there is no absolute source of goodness?

How do you measure good and bad if there is no standard (for us, from God) of measurement?

Life without God is a random life (having no inherent purpose or direction). How would you deal with people who treat you randomly? How would you deal with people who are unjust to you? With what law would you protect yourself, since there is no law for a random life?

Why should you protect innocent people if someone attempts to put an end to their lives? What does innocence mean if there is no difference between good and bad?

How can anyone avoid immorality if God does not exist, since God is the maker and enforcer of moral principles? Morality does not make sense in a random evolutionary process.

If there are moral values in your belief, what are they based on and how are they measured? How would you convince others to accept your best moral values?

If you do not have moral principles, then how do you know that your belief is superior to others who do?

Can someone be morally and ethically a good example to others if he/she does not believe absolute moral standards?

Why do you (a humanists or a New Ager) believe that all beliefs are right?

Questions about Religions

Is God personal or impersonal? (God is personal in the Bible; the gods of other religions are impersonal.)

Can an impersonal god reveal himself if he lacks personhood?

If not, how then we are able to know that he exists, speaks, counsels or judges?

How can a personal man (e.g. Muhammad) call himself a messenger of an impersonal god (such as Allah) as a personal being cannot have a relationship with an impersonal being?

If god is impersonal, how can he also be a creator, for a creator could reveal himself personally by leaving his personal imprint on what he created?

Give several reasons why a personal God must reveal himself?

If god is impersonal and does not reveal himself, then isn't the devil superior to god, because the work of the devil is evident everywhere?

Questions about God, Satan and Creation

Is God absolutely holy, just, moral and loving?

Is God the source of perfect peace?

Where did Satan come from? Was he corrupted by God or by himself?

What is the origin of sin? Does it come from God or somewhere else?

Can a just God create or inspire sin?

Can a holy God have partnership with sin or a sinner?

Where did death and suffering come from?

Did a holy and perfect God create a suffering, imperfect world?

Would a God of absolute justice save humanity, in this present life, from Satan (and the awful effects of Satan's work), or would an absolutely just God leave humanity's salvation from Satan to be revealed after death, in the next life?

Why would God wait to save men and women after they have lived their lives?

Would a just and loving God give us assurance of salvation in this life, or would he leave people with uncertainty about their salvation until the afterlife?

Would God be interested in abolishing the work of Satan on earth? Why?

Questions about Sin and Humanity

Do you see lawlessness, sin, immorality, unrighteousness as a problem in everyone's life on earth? If yes, what is the solution? If not, why not?

Have you ever sinned, or broken the law or the heart of someone? In other words, have you ever cooperated with Satan?

Is it better to flee from Satan, or to be freed from his influence?

How is your relationship with God? Does your life please God?

Do you sense you are accepted by God and do you have a personal relationship with Him? Or are you saved and close to God?

Who is able to implant holiness and righteousness in man's heart (or save him)?

Can you save yourself from Satan and sin?

Does Satan want you to be saved?

Are you more powerful than Satan: can you save yourself from his influence and bondage?

Are you able to destroy the works of the devil in your life? If not, do you then need a higher power to overcome Satan and rescue you from his hand?

If God is ready to save you here on earth, would you be willing?

Nine Belief Systems

PART II

3

Communism

Beliefs

In communism, God and any other supernatural things do not exist, because science cannot examine them via empirical means. Only matter exists and it is the ultimate reality. Dialectical (thesis + antithesis or two opposite forces of) materialism is the creator of everything (synthesis), including the five senses in a person's body.

Since God does not exist in Communism, there is no ultimate, intelligent Mind and no absolute moral code for life. Everything that exists is matter and comes from matter. Intelligence is also a random product of matter. Every existing thing is the result of evolution and is progressively heading toward perfection. Man is the highest evolved animal (in particular the working class or proletariat) and is the creator of moral law under the dialectical guide of an economic system—the force of production in a society. The economic system in a communist society determines the moral codes and the position of everything else in that society throughout its history.

Overall, communism rejects a free-market economy and believes in a state-controlled economy. For communists, a free-market economy encourages the wealthy and property owners to degrade the working classes, abusing them like slaves. The solution is the establishment of an authoritarian working-class government that abolishes ownership, rules the economy, and prevents exploitation through controlling the distribution and prices of products so that everybody can benefit equally.

In a revolutionary proletariat (working) community, the state represents the community and writes law, becoming the ultimate authority of justice to lead its revolutionary community forward. Any person or group of people who opposes the decisions or authority of the state is guilty of injustice. Freedom of choice is unacceptable in communism. It is unethical for an individual to stand for freedom, for freedom requires choice, and in an evolutionary process where everything occurs randomly, freedom of choice is an anomaly.

Communism believes that democracy or freedom is the cause of capitalism, of classes and class struggle, and therefore the cause of the unjust distribution of wealth. In order to abolish the existing class or capitalism, the working class needs to rise up, seize power and establish a workers' dictatorship (state). Only the workers' state has the right to fight, persecute and kill, until the goal is achieved. The dictatorship of workers (proletariat government) will end when class differences are abolished. Then real communism will be achieved and true justice emerges.

Though democracy is called evil and the cause of so-called "evil capitalism", it is thought to be a necessary evil for the evolution to communism. When the proletariat state is not yet established, communists use democracy in a non-proletariat society as a bridge for the destruction of existing principles, in order to establish their proletariat state. In other words, freedom in each non-proletariat community (in particular within a capitalist community) can be used for the destruction of that community. Freedom leads the bourgeoisie (property owners/thesis) to exploit their employees (the antithesis) more and more; this exploitation will eventually become unbearable to employees and will lead them to a revolution for the abolishment of ownership rights of property (capitalists) and the establishment of socialism (synthesis—a government owned and controlled economy). Socialism will pave the way via evolution (gradual and random maturation) and revolution (demonizing private ownership) for the establishment of a perfect economic system, producing a pure form of communism in which nobody owns anything but has access to everything he or she needs.

From the perspective of communism, socialism is imperfect at the beginning: it is the malignant seed of communism planted in the field of capitalism and watered by the values of capitalism—including freedom—for the eventual destruction of capitalism. At the beginning, it is less socialist and more capitalist in nature. Gradually, it advances toward perfection by prying businesses from the hands of capitalists moving in stages towards the rule of a socialist and proletariat government. Socialism will eventually disappear when humanity has perfectly evolved to its highest evolutionary position—that of a perfect communist—and can live without owning anything. In this way the fully ripened harvest of communism will finally arrive.

Problems, Questions and Answers

1. How does socialism establish itself if a society is not capitalistic? Is the Marxist-Leninist theory practical and realistic for non-capitalistic society?

In evolutionary terms, communists need capitalism to exist in order for socialism to emerge. However, the history of communism in the 20th century has proven that communists were impatient in seeking for such a transition. Communists have captured countries where businesses were fully controlled by governments, and the societies were lagging in capitalism. Stalin, for example, captured many European and Asian countries with underdeveloped economic systems and governed them under the rule of communism despite their unpreparedness for communism. East Germany fell into the hands of Stalin not because of economic maturity in capitalism, nor because it was more susceptible to the rise of socialism than West Germany, which saved itself from communism. In fact, the return of East Germany to the capitalist West is a clear sign that the communist theory is impractical. For decades, East Germany called itself a communist country, but now it has returned to the capitalism of the West because communism failed. Marxism and Leninism are only theory—bad theory; they are not practical or realistic.

Russia and China are prime examples of the unrealistic nature of communist theory. They began their own genre of communism in non-capitalist countries. Then they were forced to preserve and strengthen the existing bourgeoisies, and even advance them in a more capitalist way, for the survival of their communities. The reason for these non-communist reversions was that they needed to prepare their societies for socialism. In other words, communists needed to create a so-called evil capitalism, first so that they could exploit the employees, stir employees' anger because of exploitation, provoke their employees to abolish capitalism, and if necessary to get killed by their employees all in the name of establishing a socialist bridge to communism. What a life!? If Russian and Chinese societies were not ready for the rise of socialism, how then were Lenin, Mao and their peers able to claim the need for socialism without debunking capitalism? If there was no capitalist exploitation in these non-capitalist societies, and Lenin and Mao had not tasted the so-called bitterness of capitalism, how could they blame capitalism and run their non-socialist revolutions in the name of anti-capitalist socialism or communism? How can progressive evolution contradict itself by skipping over natural processes (capitalism-exploitation-revolution-socialism-communism) which are supposed to take time? How could a random evolutionary economic system give up its force and hand over its power to its products, i.e., man (Lenin and Mao), to alter its outcome? Eventually, we see that both Lenin and Mao chose their own preferred economic systems (contrary to communist philosophy) and thus proved that man has authority over his destiny—economic and environmental—and has a free will that is both practical and historical.

2. Why would the bourgeoisie (property owners) be rejected and the proletariat (ownership of workers) be accepted, since evolution is not supposed to take place by will-power? How could an evolutionary man foresee the real needs and interests of the future, establish principles and call upon all his contemporary revolutionaries to fight accordingly?

Communism cannot appear with pre-determined principles; it is supposed to be the random and final product of class struggle. Therefore, desiring, deciding, foreseeing or writing principles are all non-evolutionary acts which do not match the theory of communism. If communists do such things with their lives, this means that in practice they are rejecting the major principle of progressive Marxist-Leninism that societies reach their level of perfection—which is communism—randomly. So, everything in Marxist-Leninism changes constantly, not according to human will, but according to the pressures of the unavoidable dialectical wars among opposing classes.

3. Can communists prove scientifically that communism will emerge?

For communism, life began with random evolution millions of years ago, and it is still random and progressive and will continue to be until the ultimate communist society appears. Communists rely on so-called scientific inquiry into existing things such as fossils, relying on the thesis of uniformitarianism, in order to convince people of the truth of the evolutionary process. However, there are no future things (or fossils) yet and the transitional processes of socialism to perfection (communism) have not taken place in order to provide a basis for a scientific description of the future. In other words, future evolutions have not yet occurred and the science cannot be applied to the future. How then can an evolutionary mind predict the non-scientific community of communism? The idea of communism is not scientific, and it is against the principles of evolution also since evolution cannot see into the future.

4. What would life be like in the final stage of a communist society where everybody is supposed to be perfect? Will all houses, cars, airplanes, schools, offices, computers, shopping centers, roads, restaurants, foods, and all other things be the same and have similar and common capacity, color or taste? If not, how will a "perfect" human be able to be indifferent when his peers have more and better opportunities than himself?

Oddly, no government in the final stages of communism needs to exist if everyone is perfect—there is no need of a governor. This raises four serious inconsistencies in communist philosophy. First, communists believe that a less regulated or centralized economic system in capitalism is what causes exploitation and slavery. Their solution to this exploitation is to bring businesses under the rule of an authoritarian, pro-worker government with a centralized plan, because the lack of a centralized government would block the way of progress to communism. On the other hand, since communism cannot develop without a centralized government, how can it survive without such a government?

Second, if we speak in evolutionary terms, a centralized (socialist) government system is the evolved version of a decentralized non-governmental (capitalist) economic system. In other words, socialism (or communism in its initial stage) emerges when all power is centralized in a government and everything is ruled by it. If the existence of such a government is necessary for the emergence, survival, progress and perfection of the evolutionary and revolutionary communism, how then will the disappearance of this government result in the emergence of the perfect evolutionary communist society?

Third, a careful analysis of the evolutionary theory of communism in respect of government proves that the end product of communism is capitalism, which was an earlier, rejected stage of development. To be clear, let us put these thoughts in a formula:

CAPITALISM	= DISAPPEARANCE OF GOVERNMENTAL ECONOMY
ULTIMATE COMMUNISM	= DISAPPEARANCE OF GOVERNMENTAL ECONOMY

This means:

ULTIMATE COMMUNISM	= CAPITALISM

If the emergence of both capitalism and communism (according to Marxist-Leninist theory) is characterized by the disappearance of a centralized, governmental power, does this mean that this kind of communism will return society to capitalism? It most likely will, since individuals have absolute freedom and do not have social, political, or moral restrictions.

Fourth, what will life be like in an ultimately perfect communist society? Will all people think, speak and act alike? Will everyone stop behind traffic lights, stay under the speed limit, be happy to make the same amount of money, and eat and drink the same things? Will they all sleep alike? Will they all plan their lives alike? Will they all have the same capability, capacity, characteristics, behavior or desires? If not, then what will guarantee people equal rights and opportunities in such a diverse society without a sovereign law and government? Human history has proven that people are different and therefore their expectations are different. Without a government and an ethical standard, people will not respect each other's rights.

5. Why would property owners (bourgeoisie) be rejected in favor of ruling workers (the proletariat), since evolution is not a process determined by choice? How can communism call democracy undesirable, since it is the unpreventable product of its own so-called economic and material evolution? In other words, how can communism reject the bourgeoisie and democracy since evolution, unavoidably, causes it? Does this mean that communism contradicts its own philosophy? How could humanity, with its inconsistent and random evolutionary mind, foresee the real needs and interests of the future (of the proletariat) and call upon revolutionaries to fight according to a set of principles?

Communism is not against the evolutionary genesis of democracy, but against any idea that holds democracy as the provider of autonomy for people in the use of their own mind and decision-making powers. On the other hand, communism believes that in democracy, only the business class has freedom, and not the working class: this results in the exploitation of the working class. For communism, real democracy emerges with the working class when it terminates exploitation in capitalistic democracy through physical struggle. Communism holds that a capitalist democracy is only for the exploitation of the working class, and that it is evil.

There are several problems with this communist view: First, Communism asks workers to bite the hand that feeds them, to use their autonomy (the fruit of so-called evil democracy), which the business class has provided, to destroy the business class. But according to communism, it is the evolution and the power of the dualistic and dialectical nature of matter and economy that causes class struggle. It is not in people's minds, nor by their choice that they rise up to destroy democratic capitalism. Communism maintains that humanity is not able to guide itself, nor to decide for itself what happens in this life. Hence, if a worker is asked by communist leaders to fight against his business lord, those leaders are denying and destroying their own theory.

Second, if a worker (as a man) has power to decide, so does a businessman. It is illogical for the business owner to establish democracy for the destruction of his own business. A businessman uses his decision-making-power to plan and protect his business against attack. Indeed, it was for this reason that business owners in capitalist countries discovered that the productivity of workers and the quality of products are greater in an autonomous working environment. For this reason businessmen gave autonomy to workers and have even shared their benefits with them.

Third, if democracy is the creator of classes in a society, the use of democracy by communists will also lead them to the re-establishment of classes. In other words, the culture of discrimination and exploitation creates the same thing: like begets like.

Fourth, since democracy is evil, according to communism, the use of such an evil channel for the establishment of communism will also bring about an evil communism: bad motives will lead to bad results.

6. Communism claims that human beings are the most evolved of animals. How was this so-called evolved animal enabled to use his mind and write his own moral codes? Why would man refer to experiences and write laws if material evolution drives life randomly, without order?

The theory of evolution is unable to provide a date for such a transitional progress, because it is a theory and irrelevant to science and experience. Also, communism's theory about man's mind and moral law is illogical. If life, and everything else, is progressive and run randomly by matter, then there is no place for any moral law or order, since everything is evolving constantly. Also, life in communist countries has proven that the leaders established their laws and ethics on the sayings of older deceased thinkers. For example, communism in China is called Maoist and in Russia it is called Marxist-Leninism. In the evolutionary theory of communism old minds and all things should become obsolete and be replaced with the newer evolving matters, the result of class struggles.

Communists contradict their own theory of evolution when they focus on the issues and ideas of the past. The ideas of communism and evolution are not practical and are unrealistic, since people are not able to avoid the power of their own minds and decision making potential.

4

Secular Humanism

Beliefs

There are different views associated with Humanism. The goal of this book is not to address the different views, but to focus on the practical problems with the materialistic aspect of humanism, which is the belief that humanity has infinite power and is able to get along without God.

Contemporary humanism rejects the existence of God and faith in God. It believes that the world began with mindless, chaotic matter and that through a "big bang" this turned into millions of highly ordered species, which we see now around us. The process of changing from a primordial stage of existence to a more advanced stage is called evolution. So for humanism it is not a supreme mind (God) that created the world in an orderly fashion but disorderly and mindless matter, which became subjected to random evolution.

Since everything began with matter, matter precedes mind. Mind is the random product of matter. Mind is also progressive, in a state of evolution. For this reason, there is no "right" or "wrong" for whatever happens, since moral values are also random and progressive. The existence of everything is intellectually indefensible since it has come into being by accident. For the same reason, humanist philosophy regards everything as good, and expects little or no accountability from mankind for its spontaneous actions and thoughts. Without accountability we have no reason to reject the murders committed by Hitler, Stalin, radical Muslims or abortionists: everything in its own time and place is acceptable as the product of random evolutionary processes.

Humanism focuses on human beings—their values and needs. It claims that humanity has pulled himself up from a primordial condition to a sophisticated level of civilization and therefore has unlimited power to solve its problems, to make his world a better place. The Humanist does not believe that God exists—does not believe that man needs God—and does not, therefore, believe God contributes anything of value for humanity's betterment. On the other hand, God views mankind in a self-destructive dilemma—the world is in chaos (corrupted by sin and in decay) and frustrates humanity's ability to permanently solve its problems. God says people are sinners, bent on self-destruction. According to Humanism, people can overcome their humiliation without "supernatural" assistance by approaching the world historically and scientifically, using their unlimited power to ensure their own future and perfect their environment.

Humanism seems contradictory and confusing. Men and women, as we know them to be, are challenged (by their "conscience") to plan and to work hard for a better life and a more secure future. Even Humanism urges people to work in accordance with the best science and with history to improve themselves. Yet, the evolutionary human being, (the random product of evolution) is supposed to develop without regard to a plan—any plan, because evolution is a process without a purpose.

Humanists claim reason has led them to their conclusions, and faith in God, they claim, is not compatible with reason since science is not capable of describing the existence of an invisible and eternal God. Therefore, God is imaginary and contrary to science. Human beings are the highest product of evolution. They are the superior power, not God. They have power and are able to transform their world. They, therefore, simply need to listen to their own humanity, and base their judgement on natural science to determine what is right accordingly.

In humanism moral laws are capricious and evolve along with other evolutionary changes. There are no absolute laws or moral standards for life. There will always be those who consider themselves to have reached such a heroic level in their own humanity that they are consider themselves entitled and able to replace the old social orders with new ones, in order to pave the way for others to discover their own inherently true selves. This results in the continual modernisation of laws and social norms for the establishment of human unity and world peace. The social order is always in a state of constant change, since principles are relative and progressive. Consqeuently religious laws and values which claim immutability are considered dated and useless.

Problems, Questions and Answers

1. Are human beings free to choose their own destiny according to humanist evolutionary theory?

The answer is 'No'. The evolutionist has scripted his present condition so that it does not require his input or consent. He plays no part in the deliberations over what is best for himself. If the random force of evolution determines his destiny, he cannot play a role in choosing his job or his course of study, etc.

Is this the sum of humanistic practice? No. Humanists urge men and women to use their brain-power to struggle against old laws and traditions for the establishment of new ones. Thus, in their practice, humanists contradict the philosophy of evolution and return power to human beings and their wills, making them masters of their own destiny, even though in theory they believe that humans are passive and a product of materialistic processes.

2. How can humanists expect a good and just society if they lack moral standards and are bound to accept whatever happens?

According to the evolutionary theory, there is no difference between good and bad, apart from the principle that 'what will be will be': whatever happens in the evolutionary process must be accepted as essentially good. The hunger in Africa, the devaluation of human rights in the Middle-East, the abortion of hundreds of thousands of children in the West, and the massacre of millions in Sudan are all the work of evolution and therefore acceptable. So, the definitions for 'good and just' in humanism are different to what they are in Christ.

In Christ, only God is absolutely good and just. God has created humanity with a plan and has made people creative in order to rule over the world rather than being a passive product of matter. God has created them in His own image so that as intelligent, moral agents they may think, speak, act, reason, set goals, design, plan, work and eventually obtain their goals. In the realm of God, people are free to choose between good and bad. He desires people to choose good in order to have peace with God and his creatures. Not everything that happens is good in the eyes of God, but only what glorifies God and is just, loving, peaceful, gentle and kind. God wants people to use their autonomy, authority and capacity to evaluate things and choose the best, rather than becoming a slave to random nature. As was mentioned above, humanist theory is just a theory and does not apply to actual life. For this reason, its great products are confusion and lawlessness.

3. Can a humanist rightly guide people toward a hopeful future?

A humanist can learn from history and thereby predict what might be right and good for the future. However, if he does, this becomes a clear indication of his practical rejection of evolutionary, humanist philosophy, which is based on random occurrences. According to evolution, it is not people but material forces which dictate the course of life. We have already noted that in evolutionary thinking, man's mind is secondary to matter and without moorings (lacking an awareness or conscience about right and wrong). Furthermore, in evolutionary theory—the humanists' present mind-set—judgement, law and order are all inopportune, unconvincing, and out of fashion. Consequently, the mind of the humanist will be useless to direct people towards the future. Therefore, there is no value in listening to a humanist whose beliefs mean that his mind has no moral reference points which can serve as a reference point for what happens. This is one of the major differences between Christianity and humanism. In Christianity God is all-knowing; his mind is always perfect; he has already established the perfect law or standard of life in creation; and this is the perfect light for man to the end of his life. This perfect light is always new and never becomes outmoded.

4. How can someone be held responsible for his actions if the continual random changes in his mind strip him of a sense of right and wrong? If there are no stable codes of conduct in a humanist society, won't it open the door for people to disrespect laws and human rights?

According to humanism, humanity is subject to evolutionary forces which move it from a less advanced stage to a higher stage. Mankind must not be locked in to a "static code of conduct" because these "codes of conduct" will change as evolutionary processes progress. Evolution makes people "uneasy residents" in this present life—including human laws and rights—because they must give way to more "advanced" and "higher" codes of conduct as humanity "progresses" in its evolution. Therefore, people are not responsible for their actions. They do not determine things (by their mind), but the material world and the dictates of bodily lusts determine codes of conduct. In other words, the human mind is secondary to the body and is just the projection of the brain and the physical body (i.e. of the world). For example, it was not the mind of a monkey that changed it into a human person, but the natural condition and the unavoidable forces of nature that evolved it from a monkey to a person. As a result, human beings become the perfectly natural tool of evolution to destroy contemporary laws and human rights for the sake of "modernization" and progress.

5. According to the theory of evolution, the contemporary mind is more advanced than older minds and therefore can function better. Two thousand years ago, Jesus said "Do not kill." Does humanism believe that the minds of Hitler or Stalin, who killed millions, functioned better than the mind of Jesus?

Humanism does not have an absolute standard by which to determine the difference between right and wrong. For humanists, everything is right. Therefore, Hitler and Stalin were as right in their time as much as Jesus was in His time.

This is one of the major problems of evolutionary thinkers who believe it is the 'time' (i.e. the context) which necessitates hostility, not human sin or lawlessness. Therefore cruelty and victimhood, kindness and hostility are all the same for them. This means that they hold their ideas in higher esteem than the life of mankind. Since human kind is the product of evolutionary process, human life is secondary to evolution and hence subject to whatever the process necessitates, whether for good or ill. In evolutionary theory, the renewing of laws and order is constant and unavoidable. Therefore, those who stand against the new laws and orders are obstacles and must be removed at any cost. Since nature is responsible for the destruction of older modes, no one can be held responsible for any destruction when ushering in "progress".

We can see how the followers of this idea stand against intellectual endeavour, consciously or unconsciously, and desire mankind to react as brainless beings towards their theory of evolution. For this reason, they represent people to society as mindless entities, when their theory says that there can be no fundamental moral reference points in the mind concerning whatever may happen.

It is shocking that so often these leftist humanists attach themselves to the human rights movement without realizing that in a brainless society the rights of humanity cannot be protected. Instead their ideology is paving the ground for disorderly relationships, anarchy, hatred of freedom, condemnation of intellectual endeavour, the sacrificing of human life, and the establishment of barbaric totalitarianism.

6. Why would a humanist defend—even to the death—such an unreasonable idea while condemning others for adhering to a reasonable faith?

The problem lies at the root of the theory which rejects God and dethrones mankind from a celestial relationship with an omnipotent God who knows the difference between right and wrong, and teaches mankind to protect their dignity against such damning ideas. Surely a humanist knows that he and everything around him are imperfect and that an imperfect life does not have what it takes to lead itself to perfection. Perfection can only come when you have a perfect goal, a perfect plan built on a perfect standard for the goal, and a perfect pathway which carries you to your designed goal. If you overlook anything in the process from the perfect plan to the perfect goal, you will not be able to attain your goal. This is the problem with humanism. It is missing the premise of perfection: a perfect God. It has abandoned humanity to a random life. If humanists would allow God to enter their life, He would come with His perfect goal, plan and standard, and would transform them from imperfection to perfection. A genuine, just and peaceful life can only be realized on the basis of belief in God.

God knows everything and therefore gives life clarity and purpose. Without God, knowledge is limited and lacks the basic building blocks for living life. God is the source of justice and love, providing everything needed for the establishment of real peace. Without God, people will not have a genuine love and concern for each other: instead they will try to better each other which will damn any genuine desire for reconciliation. Ultimate peace cannot be achieved without God, since every individual is imperfect, different from his fellow beings and has different expectations. We need to keep our eyes on the loving, just and peaceful standard of God, which is not capricious, and does not empty humankind's mind of moral absolutes and conscience as humanism does.

It is self-defeating and contradictory for a humanist to ask anyone to accept their position. Since they believe people are the product of matter, and without any moral direction whatever happens, how can they justify a person choosing to accept their ideas? Should human beings see themselves as involuntary matter in the random journey of their so-called evolutionary progress or should they listen to the voice of their conscience? If they ask people to choose, they are plagiarizing the message of God who respects man's freedom of choice and calls people to follow His plan and standard.

7. Do secular humanists need to refer to a moral code for categorizing their behavior or for leadership?

Yes, but it is relative and man-made, even though humankind is held to be a passive construct of matter. Since God does not exist in humanism, the human person becomes the highest authority. Yet, people are under the pressure of constant change or "progress" and do not have absolute moral principles available to them in the exercise of their limited authority. Therefore, their moral codes are also progressive and relative. This means that nothing which happens can ever be evaluated as wrong or bad. It is "good" as it occurs, but it will become "bad" when it is replaced by something new.

We can understand how humanism leads to chaos, especially when the followers of different beliefs and ideologies live side by side in the same society. War, racism, nationalism, dictatorship, religious and ideological terrorism, and all other destructive ideological vehicles can grow deeper and stronger roots under the shadow of a humanist movement, working to effect the destruction of that society. God is non-existent in the hearts and minds of humanists and so everything becomes permissible, not on its merits, but by the order of those who come to power. Current laws and values also become subject to constant change and eventually legal relativism will take the society to a place where the ethical values of the most dominant man or woman will be imposed on others, and no one will have any right to speak in opposition. The dictators' decisions and views will exercise dominating and the unquestionable rule over all others.

Hence, the humanist begins in the name of freedom and happiness, but ends up in chaos and disaster. Relativism, then, cannot protect freedom and happiness. Freedom, by nature, is larger than the world: a godless man who limits himself to circumstances or to his own convenience and runs roughshod over the rights of others cannot protect it. Only God, as the absolute free being, can lead to freedom. Humanity without God leads to chaos.

Some humanists are aware of the chaotic nature of their philosophy, but since they do not believe in God and His sovereignty, they have no choice but to allow chaos to continue, hoping that imperfection will run its course one day and the necessity for change will cease.

People, who do not believe in God and rely on their own man-made moral values, will not be able to create unity and peace among each other. As individuals, we have different characteristics, attitudes and tastes and therefore we vary from one another. Experiences and wisdom show that if we use our individual values as the standards of our relationships in a society and ignore the sovereignty of the greatest standard (God and His standards), our different moral judgments will clash with each other and produce conflicts.

The way that particles or units are put together in the universe, or the way the members of a body are related to one another prove that law or order in everything is the foundation for survival. The world cannot have harmony without a stable order.

Therefore, the imperfect and progressive order of humanistic theory is against science and against God.

Let us use an example from statistics (mathematics) in order to prove how rejecting God and reliance on individuals create disaster. Since humanists base their morality on science, and statistics are a tool of science too, statistical examples can be an effective way to evaluate different views and help protect us against confusion.

Factorial is a mathematical operation in statistics, which can help us understand that replacing the authority of God with the authority of man for the establishment of moral codes is dangerous for life. Let us start this example with two friends and step by step bring others to join them and make the community bigger in order to prove that man without God is unable to create unity and peace.

Two friends' moral values can clash with each other and create conflicts between them in two ways since each one has one option to oppose the other one:

2 x 1 = 2 conflicting options for 2 people

After a third person joins them, the options for moral conflict among three people jumps from 2 to 6.

3 x 2 x 1 = 6 conflicting options for 3 people

Why? Each one of three has an option to reject the others, which gives three individual options. There are also group options for any two to reject the values of the third. So, three individual options of opposition plus three group options of opposition give six options for opposition and conflict. In other words, if these three people are humanists and do not believe in the existence of an absolute standard and therefore follow their own individual ethical standards, they have six different options for rejecting the values of other(s)—and even to fight or kill each other.

After a fourth joins the group, the conflicting options jump to twenty-four (24) with the same factorial calculation:

4 x 3 x 2 x 1 = 24 conflicting options for 4 people

In the same way, after a fifth one joins the group, the conflicting options become one hundred and twenty (120):

5 x 4 x 3 x 2 x 1 = 120 conflicting options for 5 people

In the same way:

6 x 5 x 4 x 3 x 2 x 1 = 720 conflicting options for 6 people

7 x 6 x 5 x 4 x 3 x 2 x 1 = 5,040 conflicting options for 7 people

8 x 7 x 6 x 5 x 4 x 3 x 2 x 1 = 40,320 conflicting options for 8 people

9 x 8 x 7 x 6 x 5 x 4 x 3 x 2 x 1 = 362,880 conflicting options for 9 people

10 x 9 x 8 x 7 x 6 x 5 x 4 x 3 x 2 x 1 = 3,628,800 conflicting options for 10 people

11 x 10 x 9 x 8 x 7 x 6 x 5 x 4 x 3 x 2 x 1 = 39,916,800 conflicting options for 11 people

If there is no absolute moral standard for a group of eleven (11), and each follows his (or her) own individual standard, the group can deceive, reject or fight each other in almost forty million (40,000,000) ways. Isn't this humanist (or ungodly) life a scary prospect compared to the life in Christ, where everybody has surrendered their individual, conflicting options to one another through the One Superior Option, Jesus Christ, who unites people in love so that they work together in harmony like the members of a physical body do? If we follow His Lordship, we will be the members of His body and ruled by the loving, just and perfect laws and orders of His mind, heart and soul.

The above statistical example points to the definite truth that without God man cannot have peace with others. Humanism errs when it claims that science must exclude God and the supernatural and put the human person at the center of everything. Contrary to the claims of humanists, the laws of mathematics and other branches of science would lead us to believe in God. Indeed, there is a witness of God throughout the physical and metaphysical world which logically points us to God and His revelations, and confirms our faith in Him. In God, we are not dependent on the capricious moral values of mankind, but we look to the moral values of God which are perfect and for all times.

Contrary to the humanists' theory of evolution, each individual in his (or her) heart desires for the best. This is why manufacturers are trying to produce better quality products and draw the attentions of their customers to their products in this way. People and their lives are more important than matter; they are created in a way to think big, desire the best, and understand what is right or wrong and what is great or not. They have a conscience, heart, mind and soul and cannot be chained to the random life of humanism. They need to live according to the purpose of their Creator in order to be creative, and able to live in harmony and peace with their fellow men and women.

When Jesus is enthroned in the heart of every individual, then all individuals relate to one another through Jesus and His moral standards. By following Jesus, there will not be any place for moral variations in life, or millions of options for conflict. People will be accountable for their own words and actions, and their words and actions will be judged by the absolute values of Christ in order to maintain harmony and peace in society.

Some people may point their fingers at the disagreements, division and wars that occurred among Christians in history, but they need to know the fact that if Christians are in a total submission to the will of Christ, they will not be able to reject or fight each other. The doctrine of Christ never supports such a conflict. His doctrine is to establish a healthy community with healthy individuals who are identified with His unconditional love and enabled to live in and work for harmony. As the parts of a healthy body do not fight each other, neither do the members of a healthy community of Christ. We cannot deny the possibility of a conflict among various Christian groups, but when it happens, it is be because of their disobedience to Christ. It is different in humanism. Rejection and conflicts in secular humanism are natural and unavoidable since there is constant instability and conflict in its values.

There is an attraction of life in Christ: The relationship between members of a Christian community and their leaders is democratic and participative. Freedom is at the root of Christianity and inseparable from the Christian Ethic. In fact the leadership and ethical values in the successful businesses of the world are based on the "Protestant Work Ethic." Every member in a group or an organization is a creative member of that organization (as a body), and works with autonomy according to the principles, and within the framework provided by the organization. A participative style of life and leadership do not match the values of philosophies—including humanism—which reject human freedom and deny human responsibility for making decisions.

5

The New Age

Beliefs

The New Age Movement is a pantheistic philosophy (or religion) that borrows its ideas from eastern religions as well as many other occults. In the New Age everything is considered to be divine and spiritual—everything a part of God and God a part of everything. All beings together equal God. Since everything is supernatural, there is nothing natural in the literal sense. Matter is the illusionary manifestation of the supernatural.

New Agers believe that all religions are the same. Every thing and everybody, including Satan, is "God" in the New Age. Through contacts with master spirits (spirit channeling) and mystical experiences or meditations, each person discovers his/her inner divine power and attributes, and puts them into continual practice in order to rise to a higher consciousness and pave the way for unity with other gods or people—whether Muslims, Christians, Hindus, or others. Since everybody is god, individuals have the power to eliminate barriers and unite with each other through their divine attributes and thereby change society.

New Agers believe that God is an impersonal force or energy and one with the universe; mankind is part of this God or universe. Good and evil are one and the same: there is no absolute truth or morality. Whatever a person does is "good": his (or her) existence is the ground for the validity and legality of his own thoughts, words and actions. Since he is "god", he therefore does not need to get approval from others for what he thinks, says or does: he is the source of all truth. So, in the New Age personal feelings and experiences are the measuring tools for the truthfulness of a claim but not in comparison with any set values or with others' feelings and experiences.

Problems, Questions and Answers

1. "God" or ultimate reality is impersonal in the New Age.

If God is impersonal, how can a personal man or thing in the world be a part of such an impersonal God? Nothing personal can be a part of an impersonal being. Therefore, the New Age's claim that everything is a part of God is wrong.

How can a relational man be in relationship with an impersonal God? Impersonality is not compatible with revelation, manifestation and relationship. An impersonal God cannot reveal himself in order to have relationship with others. Therefore, New Age followers cannot be in relationship with God as the ultimate divine being.

Does an impersonal being exist? Can he talk? Can he be heard? Can we say he is good? Can we experience him? The answer to all these questions is "No". The words "exist", "talk", "hear", "good", and "experience" can only be attributed or understood in the world of personal beings. If God is not personal, you cannot hear him or see him in order to understand whether or not he is good. Therefore, "God is good" or "We can sense or feel God" does not match up with the philosophy of the New Age which believes that God is impersonal. The feelings or experiences of New Agers cannot have any relevance for an impersonal divine being since feelings or experiences can be described only in the relationships of persons to persons. As a result, the spiritual experiences of the New Agers are only their own experiences, and they are irrelevant to God who is a Person.

Christian theology teaches that God is Spirit, but He is also a Person. In fact, He is One God in three persons. We must not deny the personality of God (as do the New Age and other religions) in our understanding of Him as a Spirit: He is Spirit with personality.

2. Everything in the New Age is supernatural and matter is the manifestation of the supernatural.

If everything is supernatural, then where does the word "matter" come from? Matter is natural, not supernatural. We cannot say that matter is only an illusion or misapprehension of supernatural being since matter has personality or identity. Again, since ultimate reality is impersonal, it cannot be apprehended or misapprehended.

3. Everything is good and every religion or belief is acceptable in the New Age.

If everything (including disunity) is good, why then are New Agers trying to unite since disunity is good too? If every religion is good, why don't they join into one religion rather than continuing to encourage others to join their religion?

The idea that "everything is good" can cause at least three problems (and sometimes disasters) in families and societies: 1) justification of violence—all kinds of violence, 2) chaos and lawlessness, 3) totalitarianism.

The New Age's social and political philosophy does not make sense since everything is acceptable. If everything is acceptable, then there will be no need for any law to condemn the attitudes of those who oppress others or trample their rights. This is what makes the New Age a great obstacle to unity, to which they hope to reach via high consciousness. We are able to understand the danger of disunity from its claim that each individual person is the source of every right and therefore does not need the approval of others for his or her thoughts, words and actions. In reality, unity does not take place by giving absolute authority to each individual but by dissuading him from individualism and encouraging him to strive for harmony within a community of individuals. This is the philosophy of the Gospel of Christ, which says:

> *For as the body is one and has many members, and all the members of that one body, being many, are one body; so also is Christ ... But now God has set the members, each one of them, in the body as it has pleased Him ... that there not be division in the body, but that the members should have the same care for one another. And if one member suffers, all the members suffer with it; if one member is glorified, all the members rejoice with it* (1 Corinthians 12:12, 18, 25, 26).

Why would people follow New Age beliefs, which put the unity of people and families at risk?

The problem is a lack of knowledge. People are forced to think narrowly, and in their static, individual circle to avoid the logical rights of family and society. They have not thought sufficiently about how the lives of their own families would turn out if completely ruled by the values of New Age philosophy. Imagine if you will, a New Age family: father, mother and children relying on their own so-called self-truthfulness as individuals and not abiding by any common family law. Or imagine a child (she/he is god too) in a family saying, "After this I am going to head up this family because my godhood has revealed that I should take over this position." Nobody in the family would have the right to oppose them, since everything and everybody in the New Age is right, and no one needs to get approval for his/her feelings and experiences from others.

So, whenever we have the opportunity to talk to New Agers, we need to challenge them with questions about the practicalities of life. The Majority of New Age followers, especially younger ones, do not know what they believe and follow.

4. No one needs law since every one is good and a law unto themselves in the New Age.

God is not the unique, moral and personal creator God in the New Age, but just a part of the universe, therefore, no one is accountable to Him. Every body is god and right in themselves.

What chaos! This means that everything considered immoral and illegal by law-abiding societies is moral and legal for New Age followers. A parent does not need to worry that his/her daughter was raped. A policeman should not chase a person who runs a red light or is caught speeding. Again, no one has the right to stop a person who wants to do the work of nature in front of shops, in streets, or in the yards of neighbors. We should not resist those who try to burn down our houses. Oddly, we should not protect ourselves or our children against wild beasts, since these animals are also gods according to New Agers, and their "divine" instincts have motivated them to tear us apart.

> *Professing to be wise, they became fools and changed the glory of the incorruptible God into an image made like corruptible man, and birds, and four-footed animals, and creeping things. Therefore God also gave them up to uncleanness through the lusts of their hearts, to dishonor their own bodies between themselves. For they changed the truth of God into a lie, and they worshiped and served the created thing more than the Creator …* (Romans 1: 23-25).

This is the result of living one's life in opposition to the values of Christ. When people reject God as the ultimate authority, and do not follow the moral values which God has established regarding the rights of others, then everything, including evil actions, becomes permissible for the individual and the society as a whole becomes chaotic.

The followers of the New Age talk a lot about unity, yet they are ignorant of the salutary values of Christ which guarantee unity and peace. New Age philosophy will not be able to create unity but rather it will be the cause of disunity and chaos.

6

Everybody is God in Hinduism

Background

India is the place of Hinduism's origin and development. The earliest worship in Hinduism was animistic. Hinduism was not founded on the teaching of anyone and has reached to its present state under the influence of many nations, cultures, beliefs and practices. External factors have turned it into a 'store room' of ideas, beliefs and traditions, making it hard to pin it down to any definitive doctrine. For example, some Hindus believe in one god, some believe in many, and some in none; some Hindus follow a life of privation and meditation while others tack in the opposite direction and join a sex cult; some are tolerant, others ruthless and harsh. In this way, the values of Hindus are sharply contradictory.

There are no false religions in Hinduism: all religions are good, have the same goal and lead to the same god. This is because men and women of every faith are considered to be manifestations of the same Supreme Being, having the same goal and destination.

Some Hindu teachers regard Jesus as divine Lord and His words as essentially the same as the words of their scriptures.

Hindus also worship demonic spirits, living saints, animals—such as cows, monkeys, and snakes since everything is god and from god. Even the demonic gods are the manifestation of the ultimate god, Brahman. This does not mean that every god is eternal. Some of them are the offspring of others and like all things they also will pass away.

Gods exercise their power in favor of, or in opposition to men and women, depending on their respectful or disrespectful deeds towards those gods. Sometimes gods merge into one because they are the manifestations of the same supreme reality that desires the ultimate oneness of all that exists. However, the issue of how inferior gods, who have personalities that merge with one another, can be absorbed into the ultimate god, who has no personality, is an issue that brings the authenticity of Hindu philosophy under question.

It is believed that sometimes a deity allows itself to be born on the earth in order to conquer evil and restore peace and order. An incarnation of a god is called an *avatar.*

Hindus believe the whole universe and every thing that exists, including gods, are subject to constant change; nothing is permanent. Mountains and rocks will disappear. Even the gods will pass away and others will take their places. For Hindus, each soul has many lives that die and are reborn again and again.

Nature of God and the Effect

Some Hindus take gods to be separate and distinct divine beings, whereas others think of them as different ways of looking at the one reality. A brief description of the nature of Hindu gods and their effect on creation is as follows:

Brahman (God) is a pre-existing primordial impersonal reality (the One) that manifests itself into multiple gods and creatures and is the origin of all. Brahman was born in every body, and the soul in every body is identical with Brahman. From this idea it follows that the more you meditate and understand yourself, the more likely you are to understand Brahman. This is why meditation has become so important in Hindu beliefs.

Some also believe that Brahman has two distinct aspects. One aspect is absolute, which is transcendent, non-revealing, incomprehensible and inconceivable. However, the second aspect is relative, indwelling everything and manifesting itself as a describable being. All the manifestations of its relative aspects—gods, humans, animals and matter—tend to return to the absolute One, evolving from one level of manifestation to another, and ultimately becoming merged or absorbed into the impersonal aspect of the transcendent Brahman.

It is obvious that the return of the personal creatures (gods) into the impersonal god is something that does not make sense. If the return of the personal creatures of Brahman's relative nature to its impersonal nature was possible, the coming out or manifestation from absolute impersonal nature would also have been possible and therefore Brahman would not need a personal or relative aspect for manifestation and multiplication. In other words, if return and absorption of inferiors to the absolute was possible, departing from the absolute would also be possible.

There are great philosophical contradictions at the core of this belief. A non-revealing being cannot be formed nor can it be divisible. Personal beings cannot become impersonal, and an impersonal being also cannot manifest itself as personal beings. Since Brahman is believed to be absolutely impersonal and has no personality to be demonstrated or described, it then cannot manifest itself into other describable beings. Second, a complete united being cannot multiply itself into inferior incomplete and even opposite beings (since *Shiva*—the Devil—is also the manifestation of Brahman and sin flows down from him). Ultimately, in Hinduism god becomes the cause of the spirit of rebellion, disunity and war in all that exists.

Alexander's invasion of India introduced a bit of Grecian ideology: the idea of an impersonal god was rejected and in its place the idea of a loving god was introduced—an impersonal god cannot love. Thereafter, a new religious trend appeared, which resulted in the birth of a baby god *Krishna* as a personal and loving god. After he grew to manhood, Krishna danced and slept with women. The women's hunger for him is interpreted as every soul's longing for God.

Krishna, as a supreme personal god who is the cause and power behind all things in the world, has attributes and therefore, he cannot be impersonal; he influences people by his initiatives. He is the creator and the substance of the universe, either spiritual or material. As the supreme reality, Krishna also desires the evolution and absorption of all that exist through the continual cycle of transmigration.

The idea of becoming merged or absorbed into the supreme reality (Brahman) lies behind all Hindu thought. Brahman is universal and impersonal and pervades all things, and all things that exist, exist in Brahman. Since Brahman pervades the *atman* (soul), therefore, Brahman and *atman* become identical and indistinguishable. The Hindu in this way concludes that *atman* and Brahman are one and the same. They are just different words that express the same idea. As a result, every Hindu can say, 'I am Brahman' or 'I have come face to face with a god'.

Problems, Questions and Answers

1. What is God (Ultimate Reality) in Hinduism?

God in Hinduism is an absolute as well as a relative being. As an absolute being, it is one, pre-existent, impersonal, non-revealing and indescribable. As a relative being, it is manifested and multiplied into all that exists.

2. What is the goal of Hinduism?

The goal of Hinduism is to quit the world of impermanence and change and to be absorbed into the one permanent and unchanging reality (God).

3. How do Hindus see the world?

They see the world as less than real, existing as the plaything of gods, almost an illusion.

4. Why was the world created?

Creation in Hinduism, unlike Christianity, is not because God was happy to create and therefore He desired and created. Instead, the disagreements within the Hindu god (i.e. amongst the inferior gods that make up the supreme god) necessitated the existence of all that exists. Therefore, sadness, bitterness, and lack of desire and choice were the cause of creation. That is why Hindus do not see the world as being real.

5. What is the relationship between the Hindu god and its creatures? What is the idea of 'self-god'?

In Hinduism, all that exists is the result of god's manifestation and multiplication. The soul in each individual is identical with god. All creatures are one with god, and they are god. Everybody can say that, "I am god". Anyone who does not believe in the idea of "self-god" and says, "Brahman is one, and I am another", does not understand.

6. Why do Hindus believe in many gods? How does the Bible approach the idea of "self-god"?

The reason that Hindus believe in many gods (millions of them) is because everything is the revelation of god. Everybody is god (self-god). This belief has opened the way for people to worship god in whatever form they like. However, the Bible condemns the idea of 'self-god':

> *In the pride of your heart you say, "I am a god; I sit on the throne of a god in the heart of the seas." But you are a man and not a god, though you think you are as wise as a god."* (Ezekiel 28:2); *"The Lord is One."* (Deuteronomy 6:4; Mark 12:29).

7. Can Brahman, as Ultimate Reality (beyond reality), be used as synonymous to a Hindu person or god, and as reality, since everybody can say "I am Brahman"?

Reality can be attributed only to a God that has personality and is describable, but not to an impersonal god.

8. Can an impersonal god lead and guide people?

An impersonal god cannot lead and guide people, since it has no personality (relational channels) to be able to relate to personal beings and thereby describe the purpose, goal and destination or standard of life.

9. Can an impersonal god manifest itself?

An impersonal god has no personalities to manifest. The Hindu belief is a contradictory belief. On one hand, Hinduism believes that god (Brahman) is an impersonal abstraction beyond explanation and cannot be personally defined or described, but on the other hand, it is described as everything that exists.

10. Hinduism believes in inferior gods and also says that they desire to return to the absolute supreme god. Can this transfer happen? Is the idea of inferior gods real?

This Hindu notion is not real and is completely wrong. A complete God cannot manifest Himself as incomplete inferior beings. However, even if we accept this notion, its own philosophy will prove that it is not real. Inferior compared to the absolute means it is less pure and therefore it is a mixture of good and evil, which proves that inferiors have a personality. Promotion from a dualistic personality to the absolute impersonality is impossible. You cannot say all that exists and has a changing nature and personality can turn into something that will never have personality or become nothing. For example, we cannot say, "*5 persons + 8 persons = 0 person*". In the same way, the zero person (impersonal being) also is not able to multiply itself into many. The supreme God cannot reveal Himself as capricious inferiors. If so, He could not be called supreme anymore. That is why the Bible declares that God revealed Himself in Jesus Christ with all His fullness (Col. 1:19). As a result, the idea of inferior gods is not supportable.

11. Is it good for men and women to follow Hindu god(s)?

The existence of an evil spirit (or evil) in the nature of the Hindu god is a problem. It is not advisable for men and women to follow a god that has evil in itself. The Hindu god has two opposite natures (good and evil) and all inferiors that exist came into existence as the result of a collision between these two opposite natures. The darkness or the evil spirit in each person has also come from god. Why would someone follow a god who is evil? Can a god that is the cause of evil ask people to do good? On the other hand, just as people are inferior to the supreme god, so is the power of the evil spirit in each person inferior when compared to the evil spirit in the supreme god. Why then would a person wish to be absorbed into the absolute god if it means possessing greater evil? Why would someone desire to transfer from a less painful situation to a more painful situation or from less (inferior) darkness to a greater (superior) darkness?

12. Can the Hindu god with a dualistic nature effect the real justice for which the heart of every person longs? Can the Hindu god be the source of justice for the world?

A god with a dual nature which is not able to get rid of the desires of its own negative nature and establish justice within itself cannot be a good example for justice.

13. How can the idea of rebirth be against justice?

In Hinduism rebirth is against justice. The idea of rebirth asserts that every crime in the present life is the result of the bad deeds of previous people who lived before the current incarnation. A criminal and a victim were both bad in their previous lives causing them both to be involved in the present crime.

If this is the case, then Hindu social law should not condemn criminals or reward victims. Because the idea of rebirth is not able to make a distinction between criminals and victims: victims are also criminals at the same time, since they carry the victimhood with themselves.

However, we know that human conscience and social laws have clearly distinguished between criminals and victims. When Hindus rise and press hard to gain their human rights, this means that they ignore their religious belief concerning the downfall of their so-called previous self. When someone complains against invaders, it means that s/he does not accept that his/her bad acts in the previous life were the causes of the present invasion. This criticism is applied to the Buddhists too, since they also believe in reincarnation.

14. How is the idea of rebirth a breach to human freedom?

In Hinduism and Buddhism no one is free from the actions of his/her previous existence before their reincarnation. It is your previous existence which determines what happens now, who you are now, or what you have now. Your previous existence before your reincarnation is the master of your life in the present. You cannot get away from it. You are not free to decide for your own life. Future generations will also not be free from their previous generations. In the same way when we go back to the beginning of creation (or of god's multiplication), we see that the evil deeds inside god caused the creation of choice-less people. So the lack of freedom comes from god and is passed from generation to generation forever.

With these things in mind, it is strange that Hinduism teaches meditation on "Ultimate Reality" (god) in order to reach freedom and perfection. What freedom or perfection is there in knowing that in Hinduism even god is neither free nor perfect?

15. Why does god tie itself to the world by multiplying itself in the form of men and women? Does an authoritative god need self-torture, self-discipline, self-

sacrifice, meditation or prayer in order to release itself from the world and achieve perfection and holiness?

In Hinduism, a person's soul (*atman*) is one with Brahman (Ultimate Reality). However, this so-called all-powerful Brahman existing as a person's soul has chained itself to the world and now needs to work hard in order to release itself from the bondage of the world. It has to choose its own path to free its soul from earthly ties, by way of self-torture, self-discipline, self-sacrifice, hard work, meditation or prayer in order to achieve perfection and holiness. It casts aside everything it might have and closes its eyes to every pleasure of the world, hoping to atone for its sins and reach divinity. The *atman*, working with Brahman, is able to create a newer and better person or a divine being for the life after incarnation.

We can see the extent of the contradictory nature of Hindu philosophy: the dualistic nature of god caused division and multiplication inside its own being, therefore god had no choice but to surrender itself to the bondage of inferior and imperfect multiplications as men and women, creating catastrophic events for itself which can be seen in the daily lives of humanity, all the while attempting to release itself from the pains which were the result of its own inner unsettlement. In other words, perfection made itself imperfect and now tries to reach perfection again. What a life!

16. Can Hinduism be a universal model for changing people from self-centeredness into a community of peace?

No. In Hinduism a person is the center of his or her own life. Hinduism tries to change humanity from sociability to self-centeredness by teaching people to deprive themselves of any contact with others and of all opportunities of social life in order to reach perfection within. Therefore, the Hindu model separates individuals from community and makes them unsociable.

This is quite opposite to Christianity, which rescues people from self-centeredness and brings them into a peaceful relationship with God and with others in this world and the world to come (Colossians 1:20). Self-centeredness preempts self-giving dedication in a family, society or in the world as a whole. It considers each individual above the community of individuals and thus disrupts people's relationships.

17. Can a person identify with the unchanging single spirit of Brahman?

Impossible. Brahman is not only a single spirit but a combination of opposite spirits. However, the existing differences between many individuals and between many Hindu religious groups prove that there are differences between individual souls and their behavior, so they cannot be one and the same with a single, impersonal spirit (Brahman). The effect of a religious guru or a teacher on others has proved that a person in every situation is influenced by others, and cannot be identical with the so-called unchanging impersonal Brahman.

19. Is there a fixed creed in Hinduism which can distinguish true from false enlightenment? Who is the final authority to recognize genuine enlightenment?

No, there is no ultimate authority. There is no fixed creed or standard in Hinduism to distinguish true from false enlightenment. Transcendence is generated through one's own personal thoughts and feelings. It is indescribable and indisputable by others or by any form of common wisdom, although everybody is believed to carry the same ultimate reality (Brahman) within him/herself as the source of absolute capacity and capability for understanding and distinguishing.

In Hinduism the human person is called god, but his eyes, ears, mind, heart and conscience are not able to discover the most genuine belief by comparing one belief with another. Every person is encouraged to discover the truth from within, in their own isolated way, defining and describing it for themselves. Even though the same so-called absolute god has manifested itself within every one and is the god of all, it does not have a unique enlightenment or heaven for all. Instead, everybody has his/her own enlightenment and heaven. Therefore, each enlightenment is true in itself for that particular self.

The lack of a unique enlightenment in Hinduism contradicts its own belief when it says that all creatures tend to turn to the oneness of god: oneness necessitates a unique enlightenment whereas in Hinduism there are many. Because of this belief, Hinduism is not able to reject atheism and/or distinguish a difference between theism and polytheism. Because, if every person is the author of his own life in order to create his own creed and enlightenment, his journey to atheism, polytheism or theism must all be called enlightenments.

However, human knowledge and experience have proven that:

- There is a difference between polytheism, theism and atheism; between a religion that believes in reincarnation and impermanence of the soul, and one that believes in the independence and permanence of the soul; and between someone who is enlightened and another who is ignorant. Indeed, it is the absence of a unique enlightenment among Hindus which has caused them to believe in many gods.
- The truth cannot be delimited by an individual's self or dogma; truth is abundant, unlimited and beyond the boundaries of any individual's thoughts and feelings. Everybody needs to discover it in a wider realm.
- There is an infinite difference between God and Humanity: for God is the source of absolute loving, holiness, justice and peace, but mankind is not.

19. Who is the final authority for establishing a way to the ultimate reality in Hinduism and in Christianity?

Hinduism begins and ends with the human person. Each person is the master of his own life (indeed the master of his future being after reincarnation as we saw earlier). He is the only authority to establish a way to God.

While humanity is imperfect, it is asked in Hinduism to create a perfect way to perfection!! This is impossible. The Bible says of this path:

> *They are zealous for God, but their zeal is not based on knowledge. Since they did not know the righteousness that comes from God and sought to establish their own, they did not submit to God's righteousness* (Romans 10:2-3).
>
> *You do not have, because you do not ask God.* (James 4:2).

Christianity begins and ends with God. God is good, the perfect and unchangeable standard for imperfect, unrighteous and sinful humanity. God is not the cause of imperfection in human beings. God created mankind in freedom but people abused their freedom, sinned against God and went astray. Then, because of His loving heart, God revealed Himself to save mankind.

7

People are the Creator of God in Buddhism

Background

Buddhism was founded in India about 500 B.C. by Buddha. Buddha was born in southern Nepal. His real name was Siddhartha Gautama. He was a devoted Hindu and sought enlightenment (*bodhi*) through extreme self-denial and self-torture. He was not successful with such practices and therefore abandoned them and started the search through a *Middle Way*, which is based on the mind and meditation in order to resist evil in life and gain happiness and peace. He said that he experienced enlightenment through his new discovery. His followers therefore called him Buddha, which means 'awakened or enlightened one'.

Buddha did not teach his disciples to be dependent upon a supreme being, but his later followers deified and worshipped him. There is no evidence in his preaching to show that he rejected the existence of gods, however he did not consider them important. He taught that people are simply links in the Wheel of Life; they are born, live and die according to the laws of nature. This is like a seed that lies in the ground, becomes a plant, wilts and disappears. Or like water that turns into steam, rises up to become clouds and then brings forth water. He based his belief on the significance of humanity, and believed that each person was able to save him/herself through his *Noble Eight Fold Path*. For this reason he spent his whole life ministering to his disciples so they could learn the way of success.

Buddha believed that nothing was permanent; all things were transitory and subject to change. In the Buddhist doctrine of *anatta* (which means 'no-soul'), unlike other religions, there is no human soul: there is nothing more to human persons than what we see and know of him. A person is made of the body (*rupa*), feeling or sensation (*vedana*), ideas (*sanna*), mental processes and acts (*sankhara*) and awareness or consciousness (*vinnana*); neither one of these nor the sum of them has any soul. Because there is no reality behind such a word, life is soulless or selfless: no one can have a fixed identity because of continual change. This will be discussed in further detail in the "question and answer" section.

Dharma

Dharma is Buddha's teaching, which means 'saving truth'. Buddha taught that existence is an endless cycle of death and rebirth: people are born, die and are born again. Therefore, every individual has more than one existence. Buddha believed that existence is the cause of suffering. This means that men and women may not be able to release themselves from this painful world. The only possible escape is *nirvana*[1] (enlightenment) which takes you to eternal release from the cycle of death and birth. This discussion will be centered on whether or not *nirvana* is possible by human power, the power that arises from the so-called selfless body of Buddhism.

Each person's position and well-being in life is determined by his or her behavior in the previous life: good deeds may lead to rebirth as a wise and wealthy person or as a being in heaven, and evil deeds may lead to rebirth as a poor and sickly person or

---

1 *Nirvana* means going out of misery and entering into perfect peace and happiness.

even to rebirth in hell. To escape from a painful and continuous cycle of death and rebirth and to achieve enlightenment, people have to free themselves of all fleshly desires and cravings and of all worldly dependence.

Buddha based his teachings on four things believed to open the way to a new life: recognizing the existence of pain; the cause of pain[1]; the need to avoid the cause of pain; and the way of ending the pain - which is Buddha's Eight Fold Path. The Eight Fold Path contains his ethical teachings: right understanding (of pain, its origin and cause and the way to freedom); right resolve (thought free from evil); right speaking; right action; right means of maintaining life; right effort; right mindfulness (being aware of negatives); and right concentration (on the truth only). He believed that this Eight Fold Path leads to purity; he asked his disciples to enter this path and make an end to suffering.

Throughout the teachings of Buddha there are no gods, and therefore no veneration or worship of any god and accordingly no religious ceremonies. In his teaching, he never claimed any inspiration from any god or divine power. His ministry was only to teach his disciples to rely on their own intelligence in order to get rid of pain and attain enlightenment. It seems that he did not find gods relevant to his teaching, since humankind was asked to be the master of their own lives. This does not mean that he did not believe that supernatural beings existed. He may have believed in gods but may have not accepted them as good examples for humankind, particularly when they indulged in sensual pleasures and quarreled with one another. He may have thought of them as unqualified in helping people to reach *nirvana*. This is because he believed in the impermanence and nothingness of all that exists, including all divine beings. However, despite Buddha's silence about gods, some of his followers (Mahayanists) revised his teachings with the absolutist notion of ultimate reality and presented it as a rational religion.

---

1 Craving is the origin of pain and suffering. Liberation occurs after craving has completely faded away and is extinguished.

Sects

Certain Buddhist sects began to develop in Asian countries after the death of its founder, Buddha. They do have similarities and do share many common values, but they also vary in some important areas because of the influences made by outsiders throughout history. The close study of two major sects of Buddhism—*Theravada*, the conservative form, and *Mahayana*,[1] the liberal form—will enable us to have a more thorough understanding of all other Buddhist sects:

1. *Theravada* means 'Way or Doctrine of the Elders' (Mahayanists call it the *Lesser Vehicle* or *Course*). *Theravada* claims that it alone holds to the original message of Buddha, and has no interest in any alteration. It teaches people to reach their goal (*nirvana*) on their own, and there is no one, neither any god nor any human being, to help them. They alone are the lamp and refuge for their own salvation. They must hold firm to the instruction of Buddha in order to conquer the causes of pain and reach the state of liberation. It also teaches that Buddha is not divine, as many Mahayanists believe, but just a man with great wisdom who reached *nirvana* and then passed on the knowledge of his experience to his followers. There is no god, nor any spiritual or material substance which exists by itself as the ultimate reality. The world as we know it does not have its origin in a primordial being such as Brahman in Hinduism: it exists only in the minds of those who perceive it. All that exists is unreal and insubstantial—the product of the mind. When the mind stops thinking, and awareness disappears, all that exists is said to have ceased to be. The ultimate reality is the truth that surpasses and governs all that exists.

2. *Mahayana* means 'Great Vehicle to Salvation'. Mahayana Buddhists base their belief on the interpretation of Buddha's disciples. They believe that the disciples were capable of sensing Buddha's revelation in its real meaning because they were his

1 Theravada is dominant in south-east Asian countries of Sri Lanka, Burma/ Myanmar, Thailand and Laos. Mahayana is dominant in the northern countries of Nepal, Tibet, Vietnam, China, Korea and Japan.

chosen ones. They lived with him, saw him and heard him face to face; they were Buddha's direct and real messengers who experienced life with him.

A vast majority of Buddhists belong to the Mahayana sect. They teach that people are not alone and that everybody can gain salvation by good works, and also by seeking help and guidance from human and supernatural beings. They see Buddha as having three different forms: the man Gautama who achieved enlightenment; a human being who became divine; and the absolute and eternal reality that transcends all limiting conditions. As a divine being, Buddha works through other savior Buddhas or Gurus in the lives of people to promote their spirituality.

Compared to Theravada, Mahayana takes a Hindu Pantheistic approach, describing ultimate reality with two distinct aspects, relative and absolute. The relative aspect is the representative of the absolute and adapts to earthly conditions in order to relieve people from suffering and lead them to liberation.

Since Mahayana Buddhism is closely related to Hinduism, the questions and answers below are based on Theravada Buddhism, to avoid duplication.

Problems, Questions & Answers

1. What characteristics of the gods may have caused Buddha to ignore or to consider them less important?

In Hinduism, Buddha saw that gods were self-destructive, involved in fighting and sensual pleasures, had a transitory nature, were incomplete, impermanent, having a negative effect on people. This may have caused Buddha to see them as unreliable and bad examples for humankind.

2. Can human beings be their own light and refuge? Can they put away all their cravings, extinguish them all within themselves and reach perfect liberation?

In Buddhism, like Hinduism but unlike Christianity, human beings are the masters of their own lives. He is the source and authority of his own faith. Therefore, if every person is the master of his own life, a craving, therefore, might not be called a craving in another person's mind. Therefore, Buddha's instructions cannot play the role of a fixed creed in other people's lives.

Secondly, in Buddhism faith is made in the mind of human beings who are transitory, relative and unreal. Therefore, the truth about that faith is also relative and unreal. A person therefore cannot be his own real light and refuge. He needs the real light from outside of his life to enlighten him and give him life.

Also, for Buddha, enlightenment is the state of perfect liberation. If someone who is called the master of his own life has not reached the state of perfect liberation yet, it means that he is imperfect. We know that imperfection never leads to perfection. It is only the perfect that can lead to perfection. So, people need the Perfect Being to lead them to perfection.

Lastly, since humankind alone is the master of its own life, it is also the creator or the cause and gratifier of its own cravings. How can a person be trusted as a savior while he or she is the source and gratifier of his own pain? The history of human experience has proven that the powers of temptation which have imprisoned humankind are above and beyond its power. If, on the other hand, humanity had greater powers than temptation, people would have the ability to overcome, and not succumb, to it, leaving great lessons of confidence and hope for future generations. However, this is not the case, since history has only ever heard of One who has successfully defeated human cravings, Jesus Christ (Ephesians 2:1-10).

*3. Is the view of peace and happiness presented in Buddhism absolute or relative? How might one know when he has achieved peace and happiness (**Nirvana**)?*

In Buddhism everything exists when it is conceived in the mind. When the mind stops and awareness fades away everything disappears. Therefore, peace and happiness, like everything that exists, are not absolute but relative. Even though Buddha talked about enlightenment, his 'relative philosophy' cannot present absolute enlightenment. If something is relative this means it might not be right. Therefore, no one in Buddhism can be certain of achieving peace and happiness.

4. Is the Eight Fold Path sufficient to lead someone to attain perfect peace and happiness? What obstacles stand in the way of achieving happiness and peace?

We know that each person in the world is able to discipline him/herself to be good to some extent by following a set of instructions, but no one is completely able to get rid of all evil desires from his/her heart. This will be much more evident in the case of Buddhism, which offers no divine aid and there is no power beyond your own thought to empower you. On the other hand, Buddha rejected the permanence and eternal entity of 'self', believing it only to be a figment of our imagination. Therefore, reaching perfect peace and happiness means to reach the nothingness of all and self. In other words, a person who continually becomes emptied of Buddhist imaginary 'self' cannot use the self identifying pronoun 'I' and therefore is not able to say that 'I' can be attentive to the Eight Fold Path and consequently cannot concentrate on the real truth. Thirdly, if everything is unreal in the world, Buddha's discovery of pain and his Eight Fold Path for the resolution of that pain is unreal.

5. Does Buddhism believe in the existence of any real thing in the world?

No. For Buddhism everything is unreal and insubstantial. It exists only because you think it exists.

6. Is Buddhism able to introduce a universal faith of peace and happiness?

Buddhism was founded on the limited mind of humanity, who it believes has become the cause of all pain and suffering. If humanity is the cause of every pain, his faith and every other product of the human mind also carries the pain and suffering within themselves. Therefore, humanity, who is the cause of every pain, is not able to create and introduce a universal faith which can give peace and happiness to people.

Second, Buddhism has omitted the 'soul' of mankind from its philosophy, and consequently its instructions of faith (the Eight Fold Path) do not cover all the dimensions of life. Therefore it cannot be complete in its approach to the human need of peace and happiness.

Third, Buddhism believes in the nothingness (emptiness) of all that exists. Accordingly, any idea, including Buddha's teaching, which comes from nothingness must be nothing.

Fourth, Buddhism believes that everything is the product of the mind: when the mind stops working everything disappears. Therefore faith can have no permanent value.

7. What is the difference between Christianity and Buddhism?

The greatest difference is in the area of hope. In Buddhism, when you become empty of everything and lose your hope in all that exists, you attain the peace and happiness that are only defined by the limited and relative boundary of an individual. The perception of peace and happiness in one individual's eyes will not be the same as another individual's. However humanity needs an absolute standard of peace and happiness in order to effectively achieve genuine peace and happiness amongst all individuals. In Christianity you are transferred from unstable human hope to eternal hope, from individual and self-centered happiness and peace to eternal happiness and peace which are the result of reconciliation and togetherness of all that exist in heaven and on earth (2 Corinthians 5:18-21; Colossians 1:20).

A second difference is the soul of mankind. Buddhism believes people are soulless or selfless, but Christianity believes that people have eternal souls, thus the permanent nature of the soul may link them to eternal peace and happiness (Matthew 25:46; John 5:24; Romans 2:7; 6:23).

Buddha's philosophy of 'no soul' is illogical and contradicts itself. If life is the continuous cycle of death and rebirth, and if human beings are nothing more than what we see, then which part of a person will carry itself to the next reincarnation or rebirth? If soul or self is imaginary, then consciousness, pain, suffering, and salvation are likewise also imaginary, and even Buddha's teachings become imaginary and unreal.

Second, if no one has a fixed identity, Buddha's Eight Fold Path cannot be applied as a fixed instruction to other people and later generations, since he himself did not have a fixed identity. If life is soulless or selfless, then good or bad, salvation or lack of salvation do not make sense. Also, Buddha said that everything, including immaterial things such as essence and feeling, is created by the human mind. If these things are the products of the mind, why then is it that the soul cannot be the product of the mind and remain in Buddha's imaginary file? If the word "soul" is not the product of the mind, then how is it that this word exists in Buddha's vocabulary? Could it be that his mind had created the notion of a soul yet he refused to accept it?

A third difference is that in Christianity God is not the product of the human mind. Instead, He is self-existent and the Creator of all. As a Christian, you cannot look at nature, see beautiful creatures around you and simply say, 'they are not real, are nothing, do not exist and only the mind thinks that they exist'. Their existence challenges your mind to use logic, to search and to find the real Creator of all. It is strange that Buddha called nothing all things he saw around him, but called the work of his mind—as set out in his Eight Fold Path—real and practicable despite being unable to see his mind!

8. Can anyone with a dualistic nature (a mixture of good and bad) explore their inner being and find a way into pure enlightenment?

Dualism is an arena of bondage, sadness and hostility, but enlightenment, as we expect, is an arena of absolute liberation, peace and happiness. Therefore, there cannot be any relationship between dualism and enlightenment. No one can reach freedom, happiness and peace while he is in the bondage of sadness and hostility. Release from spiritual bondage into freedom is not a gradual process either: freedom is a complete release that occurs in a moment. One moment you were in bondage, but the next you are free. You cannot say that you are free but still be under some bondage. Freedom is complete; it does not come bit by bit. As a result, the liberation in all world religions, except Christianity, is not real, since they rely on humanity's gradual effort to release himself. However, in Christianity, when you ask the Prince of Light, Jesus Christ, to release you from the hands of the Prince of Darkness, Satan, He immediately listens to your call and releases you from the bondage of Satan. In order to think, speak and act properly, first you need to be released from the bondage of evil—a powerful force in a dualistic life. As a result, a dualistic life does not lead to pure enlightenment.

9. Buddhism always regards suffering as something bad. How does Christianity see suffering?

The loving God in the Bible does not prescribe suffering for humankind. God designed the world with and for order and peace from the beginning, and not for sin, rebelliousness and lawlessness against God. Humankind, unfortunately, rebelled and sinned against God and brought suffering into life. The Christian Scriptures tell us that how God, because of his loving kindness, brings good out of suffering in the lives of those who decide to repent and follow Him (Romans 8:17-18; 2 Corinthians 1:5-6; 1 Peter 4:12-14; 5:10). God took the sufferings of the world on Himself in Jesus Christ and provided the ground for repentance and salvation for the world (Hebrews 5:8-9; 9:26; 13:12; 1 Peter 3:18).

Paul, the disciple of Christ says;

> *For behold this same thing (you being grieved according to God); how much it worked out earnestness in you; but also defense; but also indignation; but also fear; but also desire; but also zeal; but also vengeance! In everything you approved yourselves to be clear in the matter* (2 Corinthians 7:11).

With many trials and pains in his life journeys, Paul learned that in order to prove his love toward Christ he needed to go through many trials and hardships (2 Corinthians 11:23-28). His words make plain that sometimes it is not the lack of suffering but rather the presence of suffering in our lives which gives satisfaction (Romans 8:35-39; 1 Thessalonians 1:6-7).

Also, parents are motivated by love to suffer for the sake of their children so that their children might be able to avoid or escape from some risk or danger.

8

Darkness and Light are in Harmony in Taoism

Background

Taoism[1] is a polytheistic religion that arose in China sometime between 500 B.C. and 300 B.C.. Even though Taoism probably arose earlier than the major sects of Buddhism, it has borrowed many of its ideas from Mahayana Buddhism.

There are two types of Taoism: religious and philosophical:

- Religious Taoism has ceremonies that are mixtures of animism,[2] polytheism and occultism.
- Philosophical Taoism does not have a formalized worship of deities. It only encourages people to be in harmony with the laws of nature.

---

1 Tao (pronounced 'Dao') means 'way', 'the way the universe works', or 'the absolutely real'. Taoism is practised in Singapore, Indonesia, Thailand, Hong Kong, Taiwan and Hawaii.

2 Animism believes that all the physical world including trees, stones, stars, and other objects carry the spiritual forces that have penetrated them. Animism has made its way into many religious beliefs around the world and is strongly evident in folk religions.

Yin* and *Yang

On one hand, Taoism believes in the immutability and unchanging nature of supreme reality, Tao, who existed before heaven and the earth, on the other hand it believes in Tao as the source of multiplicity and all forms of manifestations.

Taoism believes that *Yin* and *Yang* are two opposite and at the same time complementary characters that flow down from Tao (god) into every inferior spiritual and material being. Yin is the female principle of darkness, passivity and regression; Yang is the male principle of light, activity and progress.

Though darkness (Yin) and light (Yang) are enemies, Taoists believe that neither one should be destroyed. To them all aspects of life in the world are in harmony: masculine with feminine, hard with soft, hot with cold, light with dark, good with evil, right with wrong, true with false, big with small, black with white, etc. Even though they are different in nature, they correlate with each other. They exist together in perfect harmony, because the supreme power is under the control of Yin and Yang, which bring all these aspects in harmony with each other. For this reason, a Taoist must do everything calmly and welcome the consequences, whether they are good or bad, because his self or inner being is in perfect harmony with Tao. To avoid trouble, Taoists should not chase the pleasures of the world and upset the balance between Yin and Yang. Instead, they should live quietly and peacefully in accordance with the laws of nature and not make any moral judgments or act against any aspect of nature to create disharmony in their life.

Problems, Questions & Answers

1. What is the major problem with Taoism? How would you compare it with Christianity?

Taoism, unlike Christianity, believes that supreme reality is impersonal. An impersonal god cannot have any mind, heart, character or attributes that are needed in order to have a relationship with people. You cannot say that an impersonal god manifests, creates, calls, instructs, leads, encourages, is knowable and accessible. No relational characteristic can be attributed to an impersonal god and he therefore cannot be followed.

Secondly, Tao is the creator of both good and bad, and in harmony with evil. Instead of rescuing people from evil, he himself has created evil and furthermore has called people to bow down to it. For this reason, salvation from evil has no meaning in Taoism. In Christianity, God is not the creator of evil. He rejects evil and rescues people from it.

Thirdly, Taoism encourages passivity towards evil and rejects human activity in every dimension of life against evil. "Evil" is thought of as complementary to "good", not opposite. Christianity, unlike Taoism, sees "evil" as enemy to the truth and encourages people to reject the evil spirit (John 8:32; Romans 12:9; 1 Thessalonians 5: 21; Hebrews 5:14; 1 John 4:1-3).

2. Is Taoism able to fight against lawlessness in a society?

Since there is no difference between evil doers and good people in Taoism, law-breakers also will be taken as equal to those who respect it. For example, a driver who stops behind red lights is no better than the driver who disregards it. This belief will eventually encourage lawless people to disregard the rights of others and dominate them.

3. In what way will Taoism block the establishment of equal opportunity and the advancement of women in society?

Taoism attributes the darkness, passivity and regression aspects of life to *Yin* and calls it the **female** gender of the law of nature, whereas all positive aspects of live are attributed to *Yang,* which is called the **male** gender of the law of nature. This has affected the place of women negatively in society. People call them shy, unassertive, narrow-minded, disorganized and hard to work with, and use these words as a subtle excuse to block their promotion in society. Though laws support the equal treatment of males and females, the enforcement of those laws will be hard because of the negative view of people's belief towards women.

9

Satan is as Mighty as God in Zoroastrianism

Background

Zoroastrianism is not a widespread religion in the contemporary world. It was the religion of the country of Persia (present-day Iran) before Islam. After Muslims invaded Iran, the numbers of Zoroastrians started to decline. Some did not want to convert to Islam and therefore escaped into India and took asylum there. A large number of Zoroastrians live in India now.

Zoroastrianism was included in this book for discussion because some believe that Christianity, like Judaism, Islam and Mahayana Buddhism, has borrowed from it. The comparison offered here aims to prove that Christianity is based on a Holy God, whereas Zoroastrianism worships a dualistic god.

Zoroaster was the ancient Persian prophet who lived in Iran during the sixth century B.C. a little earlier than Buddha in India and more than six centuries after Moses. He called people to follow the true wise god, 'Ahura Mazda (or Ohrmazd)', against the evil god 'Ahriman (Angra Mainyu or Satan)' by the way of right thoughts, right speech and right deeds.

Zoroaster preached the worship of one God, and against idolatry. However, Zoroastrian texts show that there are other gods subordinate to Ahura Mazda. They are regarded as helpers and protectors in times of hardship and are therefore worthy of worship. For this reason, some call Zoroastrianism a mixture of monotheism, polytheism and dualism. Muhammad, the prophet of Islam, also did a similar thing. He ordered the worship of Allah only, but once he also pronounced the worship of three pagan idols beside Allah. He called them the helpers of Allah. After his death, his successors removed this idol worshipping verse from the Quran.

A close comparison between the deities in Avesta, the Zoroastrian texts, and the Hindu deities shows that Persian deities are related to Hindu deities. For example:

- Persian "Ahura" is related to Indian "Asura", who was worshipped as the only Creator and God by the Aryans.
- Persian "Mitra" is related to the Indian "Mitra", who judges in the Last Day after which the righteous can cross the Chinvet Bridge and reach Ahura Mazda's light.

The Avesta clearly shows that Zoroaster was encouraging his followers to worship the God of their ancestors, the Aryans (Vendidad 2:1-16,42). So, the idea of One God is not from Zoroaster.

Also, it is possible that Zoroaster may have been influenced by Jews who lived everywhere in Persia more than a century before his birth. Jews already believed in worshipping the One True God, the coming Messiah, the Day of Resurrection and Judgment, Hell (eternal death) and Heaven (eternal life). This may have guided Zoroaster to think in a revolutionary way and introduce the worship of One God, a coming savior, hell and heaven to his people in spite of the widespread idolatry.

Two Gods Opposing One Another

Zoroaster believed that Ahura Mazda (Spenta Mainyu) and Ahriman (Angra Mainyu) were two eternal and all-powerful gods opposing one another. These two opposite principles created the world (Yasna 57:17). Ahura Mazda created good spirits and the world (Yasna 31:4; 43:11) so that with their assistance, he could achieve his aim, overthrowing Ahriman (Yasna 48:1; Yasht 19:96) who created every evil thing. Ahura Mazda is the promoter of life and happiness whereas Ahriman is the cause of deceit, destruction and death. He reigns in hell and all bad people will go to him (Yasna 30:4; Yasht 15:43).

Those Zoroastrians who believe in the equal power of Auhura Mazda and Ahriman reason that the equality of power in both gods indicates people's absolute freedom of will in choosing either. If one was all-powerful, people would tend to lean towards the one who had the greater power. This would eliminate their free will.

However, it is in reality the equality of power in both gods that leaves no place for people to practice their free will. If the so-called all-powerful Ahriman rises up to take control over people, then Ahura Mazda will not be able to unchain them since his power is no greater than that of Ahriman.

Zoroaster claimed that the truth was revealed to him by Ahura Mazda, who revealed it to him in order to send him as his prophet amongst the people to teach them to reject idolatry and to pay homage to him alone. Zoroaster also introduced "Fire" (*Atash* in Persian) as a son of Ahura Mazda (Yasna 64:46-53), and asked his followers to regard fire as an agent of purification.

Zoroastrianism also believes in the coming of a savior in the final days, the Day of Resurrection for final judgment, and a life after death in heaven or hell. In the life after death, the righteous —the one whose *right thoughts, words and deeds* outweigh his *bad thoughts, words and deeds*—will be able to pass over a tiny bridge (Yasna 19) as thin as a single hair and enter heaven, but the unrighteous will remain in hell. Some Zoroastrians believe that all people in hell will finally be purified and released from hell. Some other Zoroastrians also believe that all bad people will be purified in the Last Day, and there will not be a hell after life.

The problem arises here, as in Islam, that Ahura Mazda takes his righteous followers straight to hell—Ahriman's territory—after death and makes them go through the ordeal of proving to him that they can cross over to heaven on a narrow bridge. What is this test meant to prove? Is this meant to show to Ahura Mazda who is righteous and who is not? Does he not already know the righteous from the unrighteous? Also, if Ahura Mazda really does love the righteous, why does he make them pass through hell and taste its torture? Why does Ahriman allow the righteous in hell to cross over to heaven since he is as mighty as Ahura Mazda is? Is the so-called all-powerful Ahriman willing to release those within his territory?

Many contemporary Zoroastrians believe that Ahriman is not as mighty as Ahura Mazda, but a creature of Ahura Mazda and inferior to him. They refer to Yasna 30:3, which speaks of two opposite principles of destruction (Angra Mainyu) (destructive) and creativity (Spenta Mainyu), and say that Spenta Mainyu is not Ahura Mazda but his creature. They believe that Ahura Mazda is not dualistic but the creator of dualism.

It was in the 19th century that Zoroastrians started to favor this belief against a widespread criticism of Ahura Mazda's dualistic nature. Unfortunately, they did not realize that even this couldn't rescue Ahura Mazda from dualism. The creator of dualism (good and bad) ought to be dualistic himself, otherwise he would not be able to create opposite principles.

Problems, Questions & Answers

1. What is the problem in Zoroastrianism?

Zoroastrianism believes in two absolute ultimate beings, Ahura Mazda (God) and Ahriman (Satan), which is impossible.

2. Will we be able to call God omnipotent, omnipresent and omniscient if Satan is attributed with the same qualities?

No! They are the qualities of only one infinite Ultimate Reality. Logically, we cannot say that 'there are two infinite ultimate realities'. The word "ultimate" refers to an extremity, a perfection beyond which there is nothing at all. In mathematical language we cannot say that 'there are two infinities' because two infinities is like one infinity ($\infty + \infty = \infty$). As a result, there is only one Ultimate Reality that has the above qualities with absolute truth and justice. If God is not superior to Satan, as in Zoroastrianism, there will never be any hope for salvation, happiness and peace.

3. Is there an end to Ahriman (Satan)?

Nothing can happen to Satan if he is called all-powerful (omnipotent). This means, there is no end to his evil threats: there will not be a single time of peace and comfort for Ahura Mazda and his followers even in paradise. If Ahriman is as powerful as Ahura Mazda, nothing can stop him from entering paradise. Therefore, the Zoroastrian paradise will never be immune to the eternal presence and might of the evil spirit, Ahriman. In fact, in the Zoroastrian paradise (similar to Islamic paradise) we can see the trace of Ahriman (Satan). In these religions, men and women's entry to paradise is based on their good deeds outweighing their bad deeds, but not on pure righteousness. Each person carries some darkness—however slight, it is still the influence of Satan—into paradise. (This will be discussed in detail in the concluding section.)

4. What is the difference between Zoroastrianism and Christianity?

In Zoroastrianism god is equal to Satan and cannot overcome him. Therefore, any hope for salvation is illusory. In Christianity God is mightier than Satan, has overcome him and prepared the way of salvation for everyone who believes in Him. Jesus said;

> *My Father who gave them to me is greater than all, and no one is able to pluck them out of My Father's hand. I and the Father are one.* (John 10:29-30)
>
> … *be of good cheer. I have overcome the world.* (John 16:33)

Another difference is that in Zoroastrianism, when the righteous die, they must pass through the gates of hell on their way to heaven. However, in Christianity God is always, both before and after death, keeping the righteous away from the claws of Satan, *and the gates of hell shall not prevail against them.* (Matthew 16:18)

10

God Inspired Sin in Islam

Background

The religion of Islam was founded by Muhammad, in 610 A.D. at Mecca, Saudi Arabia. Muhammad claimed to be the prophet of Allah, who revealed the Qur'an[1] (Koran) to him. Muhammad rose up against polytheism and claimed that Allah was the one true God.

Islamic evidence shows that Allah was the name of the superior idol worshipped in Saudi Arabia; it was a name familiar to many nations. Muhammad adopted the name 'Allah' for his own monotheistic purpose in order to get people's attention. He claimed himself to be the last and greatest prophet of all, and the Qur'an as the holiest book on earth. He proclaimed Satan as a deceiver; believed in heaven and hell; in the Day of Judgment; and preached that the unrighteous would go to hell and the righteous to heaven. Nevertheless, the righteous on their way to heaven must first be gathered around hell and judged by Allah. They may be able to enter paradise if their good deeds outweigh their bad deeds.

1 Muhammad's associates preserved his teachings by memorizing or writing them down during his lifetime. Later, the materials of his teaching were collected and made into a book, called "the Qur'an".

Islam is the second largest religion in the world. Two major divisions in Islam are Sunni and Shi'a. There are also many subdivisions amongst both Sunnis and Shiites. Approximately 80% of Muslims belong to Sunni sects.

The major reason for the division between the two sects was due to a disagreement concerning succession among the leaders after the death of Muhammad. After Muhammad's death, Ali, the son-in-law and cousin of Muhammad, believed his family line to be the rightful successors. However, Muhammad's father-in-laws united against Ali's expectation, declaring that the eldest among them must succeed Muhammad. This was a major point of contention between the two groups, leading to the ultimate division of the Shiite and Sunni.

Shiites call Ali and his descendants 'Imam' (leader) and believe them to be sinless. The major Shiite sect, which is called *Twelvers*, believes that there were twelve Imams, beginning with 'Ali, and ending with the Mahdi (the 'Guided One'). They believe that the Mahdi did not die, but hid himself and will reappear on the last day to restore justice and righteousness to the world. Concerning the final day, Sunnis follow more of a Qur'anic teaching that Jesus will come again and judge the world (Q.3:55; 4:158).

Similar to Zoroastrianism, Islam also believes that after death both the righteous and the unrighteous will enter hell. It is from hell that those whose good deeds outweigh their bad will pass over a narrow bridge, as thin as a single hair, and enter heaven. The unrighteous, though, will remain in hell (Q.19:68, 71-72).

This is not just and reasonable—that the righteous on his way to paradise is to be first placed in hell by Allah. Why is it that Allah punishes the obedient, allowing them to experience the terrible pain of hell? This is a clear example of the misleading nature of Islamic doctrine.

Also worth noting are the Qur'anic statements concerning the Christian Trinity. It writes that those who believe in God as triune and Jesus as God, are unbelievers and belong to hell (Q.5:17, 73;

9:29-30; 66:9). Contrary to these verses, the Qur'an also states that the Word and Spirit of God came to Mary and formed a perfect and holy man, Jesus (Q.4:171; 19:17, 19). The phrases "Word of God", "Spirit of God" and "Perfect and Holy Man" highlight the fact that God did reveal Himself as Jesus.

Partnership with Sin

Though Muslims believe in the uniqueness, purity and holiness of Allah, the statements in the Qur'an about the inspiration of sin in humankind and Satan by Allah prove the opposite (Q.7:16-18,179; 9:51; 57:22; 91:7-9):

> *By a Soul and Him* (Allah) *who balanced it, And breathed into its wickedness* (debauchery in Arabic) *and its piety* (Q.91:7-8).
>
> *He* (Satan) *said* (to Allah), *'Now, for that you has caused me to err, surely in your straight path will I lay wait for them* (humankind)*: Then I will surely come upon them from before, and from behind, and from their right hand, and from their left, and you shall not find the greater part of them to be thankful.' He said, 'Go forth from it, a scorned, a banished one! Whoever of them shall follow you, I will surely fill hell with you, one and all'* (Q. 7:16-18).

How strange that verses 7 and 8 of chapter 91 of the Qur'an say that Allah has filled the human soul with sin, but verse 9 of the same chapter says that anyone who purifies himself will prosper. These are just a few of the major doctrinal problems in the Qur'an. First, people will not be able to purify the mighty sin that has been inspired by Allah. Second, the call of Allah is not just, since he has filled the human heart with sin and caused people to commit sin. Chapter 7 also states another similar problem caused by Allah: he has corrupted Satan to capture men and women for hell. Evidently, Allah is unjust.

Despite all these hardships which Allah himself has created for men and women, he has called them to act righteously if they want to prosper. The question that can be posed here is, "Are they able to act righteously in any way if Allah has ordained them to be sinners?" The answer is, "They are disabled by Allah and they cannot act righteously". However, even if they were able to do good, Allah has yet again laid another obstacle in their path to eternity. He is not pleased to take them directly to heaven or paradise, but desires to first place them in hell:

> *Man saith: 'What! after I am dead, shall I in the end be brought forth alive? Doth not man bear in mind that we made him at first, when he was nought? And I swear by the Lord, we will surely gather together them and the Satans: then will we set them on their knees round Hell: Then will we take forth from each band those of them who have been stoutest in rebellion against the God of Mercy: Then shall we know right well to who its burning is most due: No one is there of you who shall not go down unto it –this is a settled decree with thy Lord- Then will we deliver those who had the fear of God, and the wicked will we leave in it on their knees* (Q.19:66-72).
>
> ...*His* (Allah's) *angels intercede for you* (Muslims), *that He may bring you forth out of darkness into light* (Q.33:43).

This must be the most shocking religious decree the world has ever experienced since the rise of humankind. Why does Allah call himself the "God of Mercy" when he inflicts pain on humankind, even the righteous? Why does Allah blame people for their rebellion, if he himself has desired and created them to be rebellious (a sinner)? Why would a god, if he is merciful, treat the righteous in the same manner as the unrighteous? Is this the Qur'anic definition of "Mercy"? If the mercy of Allah does not protect a righteous Muslim from the horrors of hell, what else may be concluded but that Allah's mercy is tyranny?

The above verses have been the cause of much confusion in Islamic doctrine from the very beginning. They prove that Allah's purpose in creation of humanity was not for a peaceful life on earth and a joyful life in eternity.

The Islamic traditions (*Hadiths*[1] in Arabic) narrate how Muhammad claimed Allah's purpose and pleasure in creation was for people to commit sin. Even if Muhammad would not want to commit sin, Allah would sweep him out of existence and replace him by one who commits sin and then seeks forgiveness from Allah.[2] Allah has thrown people into the fire of sin. In response, the righteous cry out, praying for release five times a day, doing whatever Allah has wished, killing whoever Allah has decreed in order to persuade him to rescue them from the penalty of sin, but to no avail.

Allah's ordination of humanity with sin and his doctrine for all Muslims to visit hell have left a terrifying and uncertain legacy for Muslims. They are uncertain of their salvation no matter how well they have performed their religious duties and served Allah. If you ask the most righteous Muslim, "Will you go to heaven after death?" He will respond, "I don't know." Lack of confidence is an inseparable part of Islamic doctrine. Even Muhammad was uncertain of his future:

---

1 Hadiths are the writings about Muhammad's and his companions' sayings and deeds, which guide Muslims in founding their social laws and governments, and also in conducting their daily lives. According to the Qur'an, Muslims consider themselves obliged to imitate Muhammad's example (cf. Q.4:80; 7:157; 14:44; 33:21).

2 a. Siddiqi, Abdul Hamid, *Sahih Muslim.* Hadith No.1277

Narrated Abu Ayyub Anasari: Abu Salimah reported that when the time of death of Abu Ayyub drew near, he said: I used to conceal from you a thing which I heard from Allah's Apostle (peace be upon him) and I heard Allah's Apostle (peace be upon him) as saying: Had you not committed sins, Allah would have brought into existence a creation that would have committed sin (and Allah) would have forgiven them.

b. Hadith No.1278

Narrated Abu Hurayrah: Allah's Apostle (peace be upon him) said: By Him in whose Hand is my life, if you were not to commit sin, Allah would sweep you out of existence and He would replace (you by) those people who would commit sin and seek forgiveness from Allah, and He would have pardoned them.

> *Neither know I what will be done with me or you. Only what is revealed to me do I follow, and I am only charged to warn you* (Q.46:9).
>
> *No soul can know what it will earn tomorrow* (Q.31:34)

Logically speaking, we know that the pure and holy God has no partnership with sin and cannot create sin because of His pure nature. The Holy God desires the well-being of His people. He does not lead the righteous to hell. However, the Qur'an and Islamic traditions state the opposite, and in this way put the oneness and holiness of Allah under question. Any god who creates sin and takes pleasure in peoples' wrong doing and in their suffering cannot be worthy of "godness." Such a god is dualistic—created in the image of humankind and taking pleasure in the sin and damnation of others.

Allah's Paradise: Before and Now!

The verses in the Qur'an prove that Allah's paradise (heaven) previously had no tolerance for sin but now tolerates many sins. This later Qur'anic belief contradicts Allah's reason for forcing Adam and Eve out of the Garden of Eden.

We know from the Qur'an that after Adam and Eve had sinned, Allah expelled them from the Garden of Eden. Allah could no longer bear their dualistic and sinful nature in the Garden of Eden and drove them out of his presence. However, since Muhammad the situation has changed and people can enter paradise despite the impurity of their souls. How can Allah allow men and women to enter paradise carrying all their impurity, when Adam and Eve were banished because of a single sin? The following Qur'anic verses clearly demonstrate the above contradiction:

> *And we* (God) *said, 'O Adam! dwell you and your wife in the Garden, and eat plentifully there from wherever you wish; but to this tree do not approach, lest you become of the transgressors.' But Satan made them slip from it, and caused their banishment from the place in which they were. And we said, 'Get you down,*

> *the one of you an enemy to the other: and there shall be for you in the earth a dwelling-place, and provision for a time.'* (Q. 2:35-36).
>
> *Surely, therefore, will we call those to account, to whom an Apostle has been sent, and of the sent ones themselves will we certainly demand a reckoning. And with knowledge will we tell them of their deeds, for we were not absent from them. The weighing on that day, with justice! and they whose balances shall be heavy, these are they who shall be happy. And they whose balances shall be light, these are they who have lost their souls, for that to our signs they were unjust* (Q.7:6-9).

The verses Q.2:35-36 clearly prove that Adam and Eve sinned only once and for this one sin they were called impure. They were separated from Allah and forced out of the Garden of Eden. Only one sin ruined their souls and made them immoral and unfit for Allah's paradise. He could not forgive them even though their good deeds far outweighed their bad. So it can be seen that the ancient paradise was totally against sin and would not tolerate it. On the contrary, verses Q.7: 6-9 show that Allah has become more receptive in his approach to sin. He is no longer as demanding as he was with Adam and Eve. Even people with impurity are allowed to enter paradise, on the condition that their good deeds are "heavy" and their bad deeds are "light".

This lenient Allah is the very same who previously could not tolerate the one sin of Adam and Eve. This proves that Allah's moral law is not always absolute and cannot remain the same for all time and eternity. At the beginning, the moral law ordained by Allah considered even a single sin as the enemy of virtue and demanded people to be absolutely moral. But now it does not demand people to be absolutely moral, instead relatively moral which is the combination of 'good and bad', in which the good outweighs the bad. Truth cannot be absolute at one time and relative in another. We cannot call the Truth relative, because it is the denial of the Truth.

Problems, Questions & Answers

1. What are the major problems in Islam?

In the Qur'an, Allah is the creator and cause of sin and misfortunes. Sin is inspired by Allah in humankind and in Satan. Creating sin is sin itself. In other words, the Qur'an teaches that Allah is a sinner. Can a true, holy, just and loving God be a sinner? No. If Allah is a sinner, then he cannot be true, holy, just and loving.

Also, Allah takes both the unrighteous and righteous first to hell, the territory of Satan, for the sake of sins he himself has created. If Allah is the cause of sin, he himself must be judged.

The third major problem is that Allah's heaven cannot be immune of sin if he himself is the creator of sin. If this is the case, then there cannot be any difference between Allah's heaven and hell. Why should Muslims need to be perfectly purified before entering heaven; they can enter Allah's heaven if their bad actions are lighter. In other words, they do not need to avoid sin fully as long as their good actions outweigh their bad actions.

2. If Allah, as the ultimate reality in Islam is the cause of sin, how would a Muslim be able to overcome sin and its terrible penalty—hell?

It seems that Muslims are doomed with sin and its penalty. As long as they are loyal to Allah and obey him, they will not be able to remove the power of sin and its consequence over their life. On the one hand, Allah has made Muslims unrighteous and vulnerable by inspiring sin in them so that they are unable to escape sin and stand for/in righteousness. On the other hand, he has ordained Satan with sinful deceit to take advantage of mankind's vulnerability and weakness and trap them for hell (Q.91:7-8; Q. 7:16-18). Evidently, Allah acts like a mighty enemy against Muslims.

3. How could Allah ask Muslims not to sin if he has ordained them to sin? Is Allah really interested in giving people a chance to act in accordance with the truth?

This is one of the glaring contradictions of the Qur'an, and cannot be justified. It is as if a parent was to encourage his child and send him/her to steal things, but afterward, judges or condemns the child for stealing. If Allah on the one hand countenances sin and drives it into the hearts of Muslims to entice them to sin, why would he on the other hand ask Muslims not to sin?

4. Can a genuine God inspire sin?

No! It is impossible for a genuine God to inspire sin. A god who inspires sin cannot be authentic. (Perhaps such a god is the product of the human mind that created such a god to legitimize his own wrong-doings.) Such a god can in no way be a good example for people. God must be the best example of holiness that has no favor or partnership with sin or with Satan. His actions, His messages and His justice must lead people into pure lifestyles and relationships. If such a god is not truthful to himself—his godhood, how could he ask his followers to be faithful to him?

5. Why would Allah desire to have the righteous go to hell?

This is a shocking decree that Allah has settled in the Qur'an (Q.19:66-72). There is a bridge as thin as a single hair that bridges the gap between hell and heaven. Allah places his righteous followers first in hell (Satan's territory) after their death and makes them go through the ordeal of proving to him that they are righteous and can cross over to heaven on this narrow bridge. The purpose of this test, whatever it might be, cannot be attributed to a merciful, holy and just God. What is this test meant to prove? Is this meant to show to Allah who is righteous and who is not? If he is all-knowing, does he not already know the righteous from the unrighteous? Also, if Allah really does love the righteous why does he make them pass through hell and experience its horrors? Isn't this work of Allah the same as the work of Satan who wants to have the righteous in hell at any cost? Why does Allah call himself the "God of Mercy" (Q.19:69) despite all the pain he inflicts on people, even on the righteous? Why does Allah blame mankind for their rebellion, if he himself has desired and created people to be rebellious (sinners)? Why would a god, if he is merciful, treat the righteous in the same manner as the unrighteous? Is this the Qur'an's definition of "Mercy"? If the mercy of Allah does not protect a righteous Muslim from the bitterness of hell, what else may be deduced but that this mercy is false?

This is just the opposite to what Jesus has provided for His followers. He has created a great chasm between hell and heaven as a matter of protection for the righteous (Luke 16:26). Anyone who comes to Christ is clothed in eternal life and the sting of hell is swallowed up in victory on his/her life forever (1 Corinthians 15:53-57; Isaiah 25:8).

6. What is the difference between the God of the Bible and Allah of the Qur'an?

According to the Bible, God can in no sense be the author of sin. He created Adam and Eve pure and good, and desired them to use their free will in obedience to His divine will. However, they were deceived by Satan and succumbed to his evil plot. So, the cause of the original sin that separated people from God is humanity's willful disobedience to God. The Qur'an attributes the cause of sin to Allah.

Another difference is in the area of salvation. According to the God of the Bible, people are enslaved by sin and are unable to save themselves. Therefore, God saves them. For Allah, people are called to save themselves through their own good deeds though they are sinful and have no access to pure goodness. In addition, even though people have tried their best to be righteous in order to gain paradise, Allah does not allow them to go there directly. On their way to paradise, they are first taken to hell (Q.19:68, 71-72). It does not matter whether or not they are righteous, faithful leader or a prophet; they must be first taken to hell to taste its bitterness.

In conclusion, the Bible states that sin comes from humanity, not from God. God is Holy and is the Savior of sinners. (The Qur'an states that sin comes from Allah into humanity and people are called to save themselves.) That is why in Christianity people are certain of their salvation because God is the author of salvation. Through His eternal plan and purpose which He accomplished in Christ, we approach God with freedom and confidence (Ephesians 3:11-12). But in Islam even the so-called righteous are not certain of their salvation because Allah is the author of sin.

7. Why would the Qur'an call Jesus the "Word and Spirit of God that became a Perfect and Holy Man" but at the same time deny the Deity of Jesus?

The Qur'an has borrowed many ideas and beliefs from many sources, including Christian traditions and scriptures that have provided it with a contradictory doctrine. For example, Jesus as the "Word" (John 1:1, 14) and the "Spirit" (Luke 1:35) of God is the message of the Gospel that introduces Him as the full revelation of God. It also borrowed from other contemporary Christian ideas that were not in agreement with the full Deity of Christ. These all resulted in a series of conflicting ideas in the Qur'an.

The Qur'an speaks of Jesus on how He came to be a man:

> *We*[1] (God) *sent our Spirit to her* (Mary), *and he* (Jesus) *took before her the form of a perfect man…a holy son* (Q.19:17, 19).
>
> *The Messiah, Jesus, son of Mary, is only an apostle of God, and his* (God's) *Word which he conveyed into Mary, and a Spirit proceeding from himself…*(Q.4:171).

---

1 In many places in the Qur'an, Allah introduces himself with the plural pronoun *we* which is strange to the doctrine of Islam, which believes Allah is one.

In religious philosophy, God is the "Word" or "Spirit". When someone asks, "What is God?" the answer is the "Word" or "Spirit". Therefore, when God says, "My Spirit", it means "I, God", because, God is the Spirit.

According to the Qur'an, God is Spirit. What, then, does it mean when Allah says in the Qur'an, "We (God) sent our Spirit to Mary, and he took... the form of a perfect man" (Q.19:17), "A Spirit proceeding from God" (Q.4:171)? Is it talking about a creation similar to the creation of Adam when God breathed His Spirit into him (Q.32:8)? No. If it was similar, then Jesus could not be called "Perfect and Holy". Instead, like all other men and women, He would also be inspired with sin (Q.91:7-8). However, the Qur'an proves there is no perfect man in the Qur'an other than Jesus. It is because He is the Spirit of God, unique, Perfect, Holy, Superior to all, including Satan.

According to the Qur'an and Islamic tradition, all humankind, including Muhammad, are from dust, sinners and imperfect creatures, and are in need of salvation. Only Jesus is from God, in and from heaven (Q.4:158, 171), perfect and sinless[1]. As a result, the above Qur'anic verses are appropriations of the Deity of Jesus Christ since they confirm that Jesus is the Spirit and Word of God, and He is Holy and Perfect.

---

1 Muhammad said, "No child is born but that, Satan touches it when it is born where upon it starts crying loudly because of being touched by Satan, except Mary and her Son." (Muhammad Muhsin Khan, *Sahih Bukhari* Vol.6, Hadith 71, Published by Islamic University, Al Medina Al Munauwara, P.54, ND.)

11

God is Pure in Christianity

Background

Christianity is a monotheistic religion based on the redemptive work of Jesus Christ through His incarnation, life, death and resurrection. The Gospel of Jesus Christ teaches that He is the full revelation of God in order to save humanity from the bondage of sin.

The Christian population is the largest population in the world. It has three major divisions: Catholic, Orthodox and Protestant.

Christianity introduces God as a personal and living God without beginning, with absolute integrity in truth and holiness (Psalm 5:4; Isaiah 6:3; 1 John 1:5). God is pure and everything He created was pure. He created humankind and the angels with a free will. Evil thoughts, words and deeds do not come from God (James 3:17), but from a fallen angel named Satan who has limited power in comparison to God.

Three Persons of the One God

God's mission in the Bible is expressed through the Trinity, the tri-unity of three persons as Father, Son and Holy Spirit. The Trinity is not three gods but three persons of the One God.

Because each person of the Trinity has the full attributes of God's divine nature—just, immutable, omnipotent, omnipresent, omniscient; One is not any greater or inferior than any one of the other two persons of God:

> *And the Lord is that Spirit; and where the Spirit of the Lord is, there is liberty* (2 Corinthians 3:17).
>
> *For in Him* (Jesus) *dwells all the fullness of the Godhead bodily* (Colossians 2:9).

Jesus claimed to be the same as the Father and the Holy Spirit;

> *I and the **Father** are one… I am the **Son** of God… Father is in me, and I in Him… He* (**Spirit**) *will glorify Me, for He will receive of Mine and will announce it to you. All things that the Father has are Mine. Therefore I said that He will take of Mine and will announce it to you* (John 10:30, 36, 38; 16:15).

Jesus said that He was with the Father before the world began;

> *And now Father, glorify Me with Yourself with the glory which I had with You before the world was* (John 17:5).

He said that He revealed the Father to His followers;

> *I have revealed Your name to the men whom You gave to Me out of the world … they have known surely that I came out from You. …And all Mine are Yours, and Yours are Mine… We are one* (John 17:6, 8, 10, 11, 22).

The Christian Trinity cannot be equated with the Hindu trinity, which is the assimilation of three unequal gods: Brahma (the creator), Vishnu (the preserver) and Shiva (the destroyer). The Christian Trinity is not an assimilation that originates from other realities but the everlasting Oneness that has perfect harmony in perfect authority, love, will and deed. In a later chapter, we will discuss how the Trinity exposes the bondage of sin through the revelation of God and provides freedom out of that bondage. Without meditating on human salvation, the Trinity will be hard to understand.

Problems, Questions & Answers

1. *What is the difference between the God of Christianity and the gods of other religions?*

In Christianity God is personal and therefore knowable. We can understand the truth about Him; but in other religions, God is impersonal and unknowable. Putting God in an unknowable position is equal to attributing both good and evil to Him and introducing Him as the source of good and evil. When you research the origin and the beliefs of all other religions, you can understand why their founders attributed both good and evil or light and darkness to God, because unknowability puts God beyond all distinction, including the distinction between holiness and evil, and between light and darkness. If you are not able to know God, you will not be able to say whether or not He is good.

This has caused another theological problem for other religions, including Islam. They have promised their followers a paradise, being with God or being absorbed in Him. It is impossible to believe that people can relate to an impersonal God. And for the same reason, an impersonal and unknowable God cannot relate to people.

In the same way, it is impossible for an impersonal God to manifest or multiply himself into many inferior beings/gods as many eastern religions believe.

Another difference is in the area of holiness. Except for the God of the Bible, all other gods, in one way or another, have a relationship with the evil spirit and people. For example, Muhammad (the prophet of Islam) believed that Allah was with him despite knowing that he was not yet saved or purified. If Allah is a pure and holy god, how can he have a close relationship with people who have not been cleansed from their sins? Another example is that Muslims are called the representatives of Allah on the earth. How can unsaved people, who are not yet delivered from the dominion of sin or, in other words, have not yet entered paradise and therefore have no intimate relationship with Allah, represent him? Adam and Eve, according to the Qur'an, could not have a relationship with Allah ever again because of the one sin they committed. If this is so, how could Muhammad and Muslims represent Allah and have a relationship with Allah on earth? If Allah is pure, then he cannot be represented by any Muslim. In the same way, Muslims cannot represent him. Impurity cannot represent purity. However, all evidence in Islam proves that Allah, unlike the God of the Bible, is linked to sinners and represented by them.

Lastly, in Hinduism, Buddhism, Taoism, and Islam, the gods have caused men and women to suffer by bringing sin and evil into their lives. In Zoroastrianism Satan is infinite like God, and therefore it is impossible for God to overcome the all-powerful Satan and to bring relief into His followers' lives. As we have discussed earlier, there cannot be two all-powerful beings. This would mean that God and Satan are one and the same in Zoroastrianism.

2. How does the way of creation vary in the world's religions?

In Christianity, the creation does not exist as a result of God's manifestation or transformation. In fact, manifestation is not creation. The One, Unique and Perfect God cannot transform Himself into multiple inferior creatures as do the gods of eastern religions. The oneness in God cannot be divided or multiplied into incomplete individuals; it cannot be the sum of many individuals either. He is always One and complete and, by His nature, does not have a need for incomplete transformations.

The philosophy of eastern religions brings forth the issue that the conflicts or incompleteness (a dualistic nature itself is the sign of incompleteness) in the nature of god necessitates the creation. In other words, god had no choice but to be transformed under the pressure of dualism. This is not the case in Christianity. God is purely good and light. No darkness is found in Him that forces Him into any transformation or creation. He is beyond every reality and in control of everything. Everything exists as the result of His will and love. He is not the source of every creature, but the Creator. He spoke and everything came into existence out of nothing. So, in Christianity, a person is not a small part of God, but a person created by God in the image of God.

In Islam, the creation of humanity is different when compared to Christianity. Allah created the people as the mixture of good and evil (Q. 91:7-8). Whereas in the Bible, people were created pure, sinless and in the image and likeness of God (Genesis 1:26-27). This reveals a gulf between Islam and Christianity. In Islam, sin is the product of Allah who is believed to be above everything. Muslims, therefore, have fallen because of Allah and will not be able to rise up if he has desired their fall. Can Muslims resist the will of Allah? However, in Christianity people themselves were the cause of their own fall, and God desires to lift them up.

Three Key Questions

PART III

12

What is Sin and Where Does it Come from?

Sin in Hinduism

Sin in Hinduism is ignorance and disobedience to the innate divinity (self-god) that desires spiritual completion. Men and women who stick to the pleasure of the passing world and do not respect the religious traditions and laws are misled and blinded, and are therefore not able to see the truth and reality of Brahman in all forms of life.

However, in Hinduism sin comes from the ultimate reality or god. God is the cause of good and evil through its manifestations and multiplications. If sin is from god, Hinduism therefore cannot blame people for being blind or disrespectful toward truth or traditions.

Sin in Buddhism

There is no sin against a divine being in Buddhism since Buddha did not teach about any god. Buddha founded his philosophy on the problem of suffering and on how to get rid of suffering. He believed that the whole of existence is suffering; human nature is fundamentally good; it is the craving and illusion of the body that creates pain and suffering or wages war against every other thing. Deliverance from suffering is attained by following the instructions of Buddha that remove the causes of suffering from the life of a person.

However, all other religions believe that sufferings and pains in human life are the result of their selfish desires and actions. Buddha calls them cravings and sufferings but other religions call them sin and suffering. The difference is in the words only but not in their meanings. So, sin and the consequences of sin are also problems in Buddhism, and mankind, including Buddha himself, is guilty of this sin. Who can purify guilty mankind from sin and suffering? Buddha sees the solution in the heart of guilty men and women!!!

Sin in Taoism

In Taoism sin takes place when someone does not live in harmony with the way of nature and upsets the relationship between Yin and Yang. Sin is the product of the female principal of darkness, Yin, originating from Tao (god) himself.

Sin in Zoroastrianism

In Zoroastrianism, every evil thought, speech and deed is sin. Sin comes from Satan (Ahriman) who is eternal, all-powerful and a rival to the eternal God (Ahura Mazda). Who is able to remove the sin from human life since the author of sin, Satan, is all-powerful no less than God?

In the 19th century, Zoroastrians attributed the creation of Satan (and dualism) to God as his destructive agent, similar to what Islam believes. These are the major problems that Zoroastrian doctrine is not able to solve.

Sin in Islam

All unbelief in Allah, in the Quran and in Muhammad as the apostle of Allah is sin. Avoiding religious obligations (prayer, fasting, etc.), lying, stealing, slandering, etc. are all sin. Although the general belief is that all mankind is born pure, the Qur'an and the Islamic tradition believe that sin was inspired by Allah in humankind (Q.4:88; 7:16-18,179; 9:51; 14:4; 16:93; 35:8; 57:22; 74:31; 91:7-9). This therefore has confused the Islamic scholars in their efforts to construct a sound doctrine for Islam. If sin is from Allah, people therefore are not to be blamed for their sin.

Sin in Christianity

Sin in Christianity primarily means the breach of the right relationship with God and alienation from Him, which is called spiritual death. Sin against God also disrupts our relationship with each other and denigrates our role in society;

> *Why do you boast yourself in evil, O mighty man? The mercy of God endures forever. Your tongue devises evil, like a sharp razor, working deceitfully* (Psalm 52:1-2).
>
> *I have sinned against Heaven* (God) *and before you* (man) (Luke 15:21).

In Christianity, the first man and woman sinned against God and departed from Him, falling into Satan's grasp. Satan, unlike God, does not believe in the freedom of choice. He uses all possible options to bind people to himself. That is why he is called "Satan" or "the Deceiver". So, in this way, man and woman exposed themselves and their offspring to every evil thought, word and deed and became spiritually lost or dead—unable to save themselves. They became evil doers and self-centered, incapable of having a genuine relationship with God and others. They needed a Savior who could release them from Satan, bringing them back to their initial state. Only God could save them.

Unlike all other religions, in Christianity sin does not come from God but from Satan. In Christianity, Satan is not a part of God, whereas he is a part of god in eastern religions. Satan was not made a sinner by God, as is the case with Islam. Instead, he was a good angel, created by God with free will like all other angels, in order to obey the sovereignty of God and be in harmony with His divine love for all other creatures. However, Satan (Lucifer was his previous name) became proud, desired to be independent of God (to be his own god) and therefore rebelled against the sovereignty of God and His love. His rebellious act caused him to descend from the kingdom of love. Satan's rebellion (he enticed other angels to join him) caused him to be cast out of heaven, to loose his angelic status and to become the head of a hateful army of fallen angels who wage war against God and his creation. The Bible describes his situation—how he fell from his glory and caused mankind to fall as well:

> *How you are fallen from the heavens, O shining star, son of the morning! How you are cut down to the ground, you who weakened the nations! For you have said in your heart, I will go up to the heavens, I will exalt my throne above the stars of God; I will also sit on the mount of the congregation, in the sides of the north. I will go up above the heights of the clouds; I will be like the Most High. Yet you shall be brought down to hell, to the sides of the Pit* (Isaiah 14: 12-15).

> *So says the Lord Jehovah: You seal the measure, full of wisdom and perfect in beauty. You have been in Eden the garden of God; … You were the anointed cherub that covers, and I had put you in the holy height of God where you were; … You were perfect in your ways from the day that you were created, until iniquity was found in you. … you have sinned. So I cast you profaned from the height of God, and I destroy you, O covering cherub, … Your heart was lifted up because of your beauty; you have spoiled your wisdom because of your brightness. I will cast you to the ground; I will put you before kings, that they may behold you. By the host of your iniquities, by the iniquity of your trade, you have profaned your holy places; so I brought a fire from your midst; it shall devour you, and I will give you for ashes on the earth, before the eyes of all who see you. All who know you among the peoples shall be astonished at you; you shall be terrors, and you will not be forever* (Ezekiel 28: 12-19).

> *He said* (Jesus) *to them, I saw Satan fall from Heaven like lightning* (Luke 10:18).
>
> *And those angels not having kept their first place, but having deserted their dwelling-place, He has kept in everlasting chains under darkness for the judgment of a great Day* (Jude 6).

So, in Christianity, Satan has his own personal identity and therefore, adversity and sin do not come from God. God is Holy, and in no way can sin be linked to the Holy God. The first man and woman followed Satan (Romans 5:12; 1 Corinthians 15:21-22) and exercised their choice against God, which led them and their household to a state of godlessness and isolation (Genesis 3).

A Clear Similarity

Sin seems to be a big problem in all religions. It has its root in the heart of people right from the very beginning of creation. Every religion gives instructions to its followers to avoid sin and its consequences.

Big Differences

The major differences between Christianity and other world religions are in the following three areas:

1. *The origin of sin:* According to the Bible, sin did not originate with God. However, in other religions, sin originated from their supreme beings (gods).

2. *The source of salvation:* In Christianity, people cannot save themselves since they are in the bondage of Satan. Only God can save them from Satan. Unlike Christianity, all other world religions have imprisoned them and required them to save themselves. This is impossible. Sinfulness cannot lead to sinlessness. People cannot be their own savior. Jesus said;

    > *The man who walks in the dark does not know where he is going. Put your trust in the light while you have it, so that you may become sons of light.* (John 12:35c-36b)

3. *The purity of Jesus:* All divine beings,[1] prophets and gurus in other religions are sinful, but Jesus Christ is sinless. For this reason, He speaks of Himself as the eternal Way, Life, Light, and Truth by whom many may ascend to heaven.

Problems, Questions & Answers

1. According to the world's religions, who is responsible for all injustice and iniquities in the world?

In all other religions, except Christianity, gods are the cause of all sin and injustice. All inhumane thoughts and evil actions have been inspired by the gods.

2. Why would people be held responsible for their wrong doings if they were not the major cause of them?

If gods are the cause of all wrong doings, it would not make sense for people to be held responsible.

3. Why is the God of the Bible trustful but the gods of other religions are not?

In all other religions the issue of "good and bad" goes back to the time before creation. The eastern gods had partnership with the devil, and therefore were not immune to evil thoughts and acts. Also, Allah, the god of Islam, caused Satan to err and made humanity vulnerable to sin. So, these gods themselves were not free of evil to stand for good and create a purely good creature. How then could their creatures be free and have free will? That is why they created man and woman in their own likeness—sinners and fallible—without the ability to choose truth or establish themselves in truth. If people are surrendered to sin and Satan they can no longer have freedom. Satan is the enemy of freedom.

---

1 In all other religions' scriptures, sin flows down or is inspired from god into humanity. In other words, this means that "god is a sinner". Because, the inspiration of sin also is a sin in itself.

In the Bible, sin originated from Satan and penetrated into Adam and Eve after the creation and it is not eternal as it is in all other world religions. God is eternally pure; in His purity He desired to have pure men and women, free of evil;

> *For God has not called us to uncleanness* (impurity), *but in sanctification* (holiness) (1 Thessalonians 4:7).

> *But the wisdom that is from above is first truly pure, then peaceable, gentle, easy to be entreated, full of mercy and good fruits, without partiality and without hypocrisy* (James 3:17).

All these verses teach that the God of the Bible is trustworthy.

4. Why would the God of the Bible create humankind with free will?

God, in His nature, is absolutely free. In accordance with His free nature He desired to give humankind free will. So, the free nature of God is the cause of free will in His creation.

When we talk about the creation of humanity with free will, it does not mean that this free will can only decide between good and bad. So often we only associate free will with the question, "What are we going to choose or follow?" It is first about our identity: "who we are" or "where we stand". This is what leads us to the choices we make (read the next question).

If the beginning of human beings was devoid of purity and based on dualism—like all other world religions—people would be unable to exercise free will, since evil is against it. It is for this reason that the right of free will is totally absent in the doctrine of humankind in all other religions. People claim to have it because it is the desire of their hearts, but it is not the desire of their gods. In other words, their gods ignore the cry of their hearts, because they are not real gods but the gods of humanity's making.

How can a god create evil if he himself is not evil? If a god is good, why would he create evil for the destruction of his own creatures and kingdom? They, in one way or another, have a connection with evil, which is evident in their thoughts, words and actions. This being the case, their followers could not stand for the truth. So they cannot say, "We chose to be bad." It was their gods who were bad and created their creatures as evil doers. However, as we have discussed earlier, such gods cannot exist—they are man-made gods. Therefore, they are fallible, capricious and lack free will. Only in Christianity is the Creator completely distanced from any evil. He created people in accordance with His holy nature, so that they could have "free will".

5. Is this free will a sign of God's incapacity to create infallible beings?

God did not create Adam and Eve (the first man and woman) as fallen or sinful, as other religions state that their gods did. He created them pure and in harmony with His holiness (1 Thessalonians 4:7-8). God did not create them equal with Himself in leadership and as omniscient people, who could influence God and know the full depth of His glory, love and grace. Instead, He chose to give them free will with the ability to search and understand and live in harmony and according to attributes of God. On the other hand, there was no pressure on them to live with God, because they were gifted with a "free will". Their free will gave them the choice to decide whether or not they wished to be a part of God's kingdom and led by Him.

The gift of "free will" brought them face to face with a variety of choices. It was to assist them to understand and to appreciate the full value of the life God had given them. Options and choices require curiosity, investigation and decision-making. It is obvious that there are always temptations involved with different options. Temptation is not sin; it provides an opportunity for people to discern between Satan's values and God's greater values, to allow the Spirit of God to transform them from their present situation to a higher spiritual level. However, if people do not think objectively and for eternity, they will fall short of the will of God in their confrontation with temptation and they will suffer eternal loss. The scriptures promise that the power of temptation is not beyond the capacities of people and women who are united with God and have become part of His family:

> *No temptation has taken you but what is common to man; but God is faithful, who will not allow you to be tempted above what you are able, but with the temptation also will make a way to escape, so that you may be able to bear it* (1 Corinthians 10:13).

> *He is able to rescue those who are being tempted* (Hebrew 2:18b).

For God, the main purpose of allowing humankind to encounter temptation was not that they should be separated from Him or be alienated from Him. Instead, it was so that they would understand that God is in control of every thing. People, therefore, need to abide in Him with increasing maturity, knowledge, confidence and loyalty, in order to overcome all temptations. So, with God, it is impossible for people to be defeated by temptation.

The gift of "free will" was to allow people to discover the significance of his place in God's kingdom and the extent of God's love towards him. This intimate relationship with God is the source of confidence and eternal joy. When people are tempted they are forced to exercise their free will through thinking, comparing and searching, hopefully, in God's Word where they will find wonderful messages of direction for freedom. If we want to put this message in our own words, it might be as follows;

> *I* (God) *have had a creative purpose by giving you the gift of "free will". I will lead you into a deeper understanding of things and ultimately to my greatness. I am perfect, so, treasure me above all others and all else; follow me and rejoice in me.*

So, this is the motivation behind "free will". People must go through many experiences in order to understand the greatness of God and with open eyes treasure Him above every other thing. They are expected to discover the full scope of God's transformational purpose through His gift of free will in order that they might be victorious over temptation and be transformed to a higher glory.

The transformational purpose of God in temptation comes to light in the story of Jesus confronting Satan. The firm standing of Christ against the suggested options of Satan fully illustrates God's expectation of every person's attitude towards temptation. Satan maliciously tempted Jesus to eat the bread, to provide for Himself, and not trust in God (Matthew 4:3), to presumptuously throw Himself down from an elevated position, tempting the Lord (v.6) and to surrender His heavenly Kingdom of Light to rule over the world—Satan's Kingdom of Darkness (v.9). As a result of His refusal, Jesus proved that people are to overcome temptation by relying on every word that comes from the mouth of God (v.4), by firmly standing in the heavenly and perfect position that God has placed him (v.7) and by worshipping only the King of kings, the Creator of the universe (v.10). For all those who turn away from God's counsel, who purpose to go their own way, their confrontation with temptation will end in failure. This was why Adam and Eve fell and lost the perfect life God had provided them.

God expected Adam and Eve to follow Him in all aspects of their lives. He respected their "free will", but He did not want their free will to lead them to destruction. Therefore, He warned them of the consequence of any ungodly choices they might have made (Genesis 2:17). And He never stopped them from facing temptation as it would not be in accord with the essence of free will. Rather, He desired to have His presence go with them and become victorious against the ungodly choices.

This is the key for a successful life with God: when God helps you, temptation cannot overcome you; instead it becomes a tool for making your faith grow stronger in Him. To make a long story short, Adam and Eve made the same mistake Satan did. They relied on their limited self-knowledge and met disaster.

So, the right to "free will" is not evidence of God's inability to create infallible beings. Instead, it is evidence of God's ability to prove that if a person treasures God above all (as Jesus did) he will have a victorious life. "Free will" is to lead people to the full capacity of life with and in God.

Just as a parent desires to have a child, bring him (or her) into life, feed and help him to grow in maturity so does the loving God for His people. There is no parent in the history of mankind who wants to have a child remain an infant forever, unable to learn and unable to grow into a mature adult. There is no parent who wants a child to violate their family values or bring shame on the family name. If a father or mother with a limited ability and love does not desire these things for his or her child, how could a perfect God, with His immeasurable love, desire anything less for His people?

Unlike all other gods, God did not create human beings a sinners or corruptors. He created them good and sinless, desired them to obey His perfect values, learn and grow more in His goodness, enjoy life with his Creator and live in peace with others. However, humanity ignored God and chose to go a different way from what God had intended in the beginning, a way that has since demonstrated that people are lost and aliens to peace and joy.

13

What is Human Destiny?

Where are people Heading?
Is people certain of their salvation?
Can a dualistic God save?

Hinduism

In Hinduism, those who do good will become good, and those who do evil will become evil after a rebirth. Each soul has many lives; it has no independent identity. Therefore, there is not a Day of Judgment as in Christianity, Islam or Zoroastrianism in which the soul is rewarded or punished once for all eternity. Rather, in Hinduism, each soul is rewarded or punished many times. However, the ultimate hope of a Hindu is a complete release from the Wheel of Rebirth and absorption into Ultimate Reality. Only the most spiritual Hindus can escape from the Wheel of Rebirth and merge with the Absolute.

Unlike Christianity, the hope for promotion to a happier life according to Hindu philosophy lies not in the present life but in the next incarnation. In Christianity, when you believe in Christ you become sure that you have reached to spiritual nobility and are in the kingdom of heaven for all eternity. You know what lies ahead in your future. This is in contrast to Hinduism, where you are uncertain of any spiritual promotion in this present life. You cannot be certain about your future. All you have is a collection of religious theories that bind you to an uncertain future. There is nothing in Hinduism that can become a light for people regarding their salvation and future life.

Buddhism

Buddha teaches that every person should meditate on eliminating desire and on the eradication of individuality in order to get rid of suffering and thus gain Nirvana—a state of perfect peace and happiness.

In Buddhism, the cost of eliminating suffering is to reach the complete nothingness of everything, known as 'emptiness'. The notion of emptiness helps a person to release him/herself from any dependency on any person or thing. Since everything is temporary and impermanent, one's existence cannot be absolute but is relative and empty of self-reality. Therefore, if people focus on the material or physical (or even desires of oneself), which in Buddhism are unreal or empty things, they will cause themselves suffering. But if they detach themselves from all these things, the sufferings will be replaced with happiness and peace.

Buddha left his baby son, his wife and whole family because he believed his partnership with them was the cause of his suffering and therefore a stumbling block towards reaching enlightenment. He wanted to release himself from any attachment to his family in order to gain peace and happiness. However, contrary to his teaching, Buddha was still keen on maintaining a close relationship with others. This is evident since towards the end of his life he went back to his family and led them to his faith.

It is difficult to define Nirvana—the state of happiness and peace—because Buddhists believe in the impermanence of an individual being and reject the existence of a 'soul, self or ego'[1]. If

1 For Buddhists, believing in a human soul is an obstacle to enlightenment, because it produces every kind of selfish desire, which leads to suffering and hinders people attaining enlightenment.

the self is not real, it will also be difficult to find a real definition for Nirvana. Buddhists believe that Nirvana is an experience of absorption in peace and happiness that cannot be described in words; it is an experience. Buddha himself lived it but was not able to describe it; he only described the way of achieving it.

Taoism

In Taoism, salvation is obtained through passivity – taking no action or making no moral judgments about good or evil, which is supposed to open the way for harmony between two opposite characters in life. With this passive approach, Taoists try to reconcile the dual forces of all life and creation, Yin and Yang, and in this way be in unity with Tao and hence reach salvation. Contrary to the true meaning of salvation the Taoist salvation is gained through creating harmony between bad and good, but not through overcoming bad with good.

Believing in harmony between good and bad is not just a failure in spirituality but also in every aspect of daily life. How can humans survive in a world where the unjust lives side by side with the just? The just will never survive if they are to sit back and allow injustice to take its course.

Zoroastrianism

Zoroastrianism believes that life is a battleground between good (God) and bad (Satan) and people have to accept them both. It calls upon people to choose the best between the two eternal spirits of good (God) and bad (Satan).

Zoroastrianism says that wise people are those who choose God and follow Zoroaster's instructions of right thoughts, speech, and deeds in order to enter paradise after death in the Day of Judgment. But unwise people follow Satan and enter hell.

However, there are some Buddhists who believe that they have something similar to a soul that enjoys the blessings of the life on earth or goes to paradise.

However, as discussed earlier, the theory of attributing omnipotence (all-powerfulness) to Satan or the creation of Satan to God in Zoroastrianism gives no way for the exercising of free will. Free will is what enables people to choose the best and ultimately salvation. Because God is not greater than Satan or he is the creator of sin in Zoroastrianism, he is therefore unable to abolish Satan's schemes against free will, and people will not have access to salvation.

Islam

In Islam, the righteous and unrighteous are taken to hell (Q.19:68-72); then from hell the righteous might go to paradise (heaven) and be with Allah, while the unrighteous stay in hell. The ultimate decision belongs to Allah; if he wishes to have unrighteous people in paradise and righteous people in hell, he will do so. Muslims, therefore, are not certain about their future. Despite this, they still believe that they have to try hard to make Allah happy by fulfilling his law (the pillars of Islam) in their life on earth. The general belief about the release from the penalty of sin on the Day of Judgment is when a Muslim's good deeds outweigh his/her bad deeds. The problem with this is whether there can be good deeds in Islam when Allah is the creator of all sin and evil.

However, if a Muslim enters Allah's paradise, he will be given many maidens (Q.2:25; 44:51-52; 52:17-19).

Christianity

In Christianity, God is the author of salvation. Because of our fallen nature (sinful nature), we are not able to attain purity in our own strength. We need the Pure One to take us out of impurity and place us into purity. God is not illogical. He does not ask sinners, who are spiritually dead and unable, to save (or give life to) themselves like all other religions do. God is the only Savior. This is one of the major differences between Christianity and other religions.

In Christianity, God loves to save sinners and He therefore calls them so He may save them. If people refuse God's invitation, they will remain in the kingdom of death and darkness. After they die, they enter hell for all eternity.

Unsaved people are also not able to reject or give up evil thoughts, words and deeds in their relationships, no matter how much they long to have peace with others, because they are still under the bondage of satanic influence. They might be able to use the good part of their dualistic life in order to show friendliness and peace to others, but it will not last long because of the opposing forces within them.

However, those who are saved by God are joined with God and will certainly go to heaven to be with Him forever. Those who are not saved are separated from God and will certainly go to hell.

Christianity teaches that human beings live only once on the earth and so have only one chance in their life on earth to be saved. Unlike other world religions, the Gospel of Jesus Christ teaches that salvation is a one-time experience in this present life on earth. In other words, people need to allow God, who is the source of eternal peace and happiness, into their lives while they are on the earth. Then they will be transferred from the kingdom of darkness into the kingdom of light, which is characterized by the Spirit of love, joy, peace, patience, kindness, goodness, faithfulness, gentleness and self-control even as they live on earth. Just as the sun throws light upon the reality of our world, so the Kingdom of light enlightens the realities of the world to come. The Spirit of light gives birth to a new life on earth and relates that life to the ultimate glory of eternal life in heaven. So in Christianity, the hope of promotion is absolute and has its eternal root in this present life. Paul, the Apostle of Jesus Christ said;

> *Our citizenship is in Heaven* (Philippians 3:20a).

Those, *whose names are in the Book of Life* (Philippians 4:3c), no longer belong to the kingdom of darkness and hell.

Problems, Questions & Answers

1. Why should anyone chose to believe in God?

All religious groups commonly believe that people should try their best to achieve complete peace and happiness. The cries of the human soul, the crisis among nations, and throughout the world, all prove that every one wants a world of perfect peace and happiness. The Bible says that God is the source of peace, happiness and comfort. Why should anyone remain (through unbelief) in the dilemma of this present evil world with evil-doers.

2. Are all religions heading towards the same goal?

No!

3. What is the difference between the Savior in Christianity and in other religions?

In Christianity, sin has entered into the world through humankind who was deceived by Satan and ***God is the Savior***, but in other religions god has created sin and ***humanity is the savior***. In other religions humanity has been deceived by the so-called all-powerful gods, and then been asked to save himself. No person with his limited power is able to free himself from the chains of an "all-powerful god." That is why the salvation in other religions is uncertain. The instruction of Christianity is reasonable: God is pure and therefore can save; the salvation of the pure God is better than the salvation of corrupted humanity, or of corrupting gods.

In Christianity salvation and entry to heaven occurs in this life. Mankind is provided with the opportunity to taste the heavenly life (peace, kindness, love, forgiveness, etc.) in this life. Other religions teach people that entry into heaven (paradise or enlightenment) can only occur after death.

4. What is the difference between the ultimate stage of salvation in Christianity and other religions?

In Christianity humanity returns to its purest form and has an eternal relationship with a Holy God. In other religions, gods are the mixture of "good and evil" or the creators of evil. Their heavens (or paradises) also will be like them. Therefore, if someone aims to reach a dualistic god, he will end up in a dualistic heaven completely opposite to the peace and happiness he was striving to gain.

5. How would a Hindu describe that he is released (saved) from reincarnation and merged into supreme reality?

The release from reincarnation is a very personal matter in Hinduism and describable only by the person; you are the savior of your own soul and it is for you to describe it. Hindus say that the experience of release is of such a kind that you become quite certain as to whether it has taken place within you. You not only feel that you have reached the fullness of Brahman but you know it. When you become certain of your release, you then go and help others to prepare themselves for salvation after reincarnation.

However, salvation cannot be a single individual's experience since god, Brahman, is made up of many gods, both good and bad. For example, if a Hindu says that he is saved, it can also mean that he is not saved. Secondly, getting released from the lower level of reincarnation and being absorbed into higher levels and eventually into ultimate reality, Brahman, means that you have reached the highest level of dualism since the head god represents the combination of highest level of good and bad. In other words, a Hindu will gradually loose his certainty as much as he gets closer to the god of dualism. Dualism is the sign of impurity and uncertainty.

6. Is salvation in Hinduism genuine salvation?

Genuine salvation has spiritual, logical and universal values (standard) that peacefully relate a person to a wider community or world and to God who is the source of absolute peace and goodness. People will be able to see the positive changes in their lives. Therefore, salvation must be described either by a person who is saved or by his community of salvation or even by unsaved people. In other words, people will be able to see the qualities (or fruits) of salvation in their lives. Is this the case in Hinduism? No. In Hinduism only a person can describe his salvation, whether or not others see the qualities of salvation in him. This cannot be called a real salvation. The real must be tested in the context of the world, not within a person. Secondly, salvation, which is called the absorption of an inferior being (god) into the supreme god, is not possible since the inferior god is personal unlike the supreme god who is impersonal. A personal thing cannot become impersonal and vice versa. Therefore, a Hindu who believes that he has been released from reincarnation and absorbed into Ultimate Reality cannot be real.

7. For Buddha, all that exists, including humankind, are unreal and empty of self. If humanity is unreal and empty, how then does this emptiness break the chain of suffering to reach the fullness of enlightenment? How can emptiness express on one side its release from full suffering and on the other the full joy of peace and happiness in enlightenment?

The emptiness is meaningless. It is nothing and goes nowhere. Dismantling men and women from their souls, hinders them from any promotion towards perfection. A soulless person is like a stone, which does not have any perception of the heat on a sunny day or the chill on a cold day. This might be a reason why the Buddhists claim they are not able to communicate Nirvana, because without a soul even perfect happiness is meaningless.

8. In what way is Buddha's 'soulless' philosophy irrational and contradictory to his own doctrine?

The fact that Buddha made an effort to discover a solution to the restlessness of the human soul is clear proof that he was living in contradiction to his selfless theory. After claiming that he received

Nirvana, Buddha developed a belief through which people's lives might take on purpose and significance so that their souls could be promoted. He continually used the pronouns 'I' in order to identify his new experience, Nirvana, and 'You' in order to encourage others to reach this stage. These pronouns refer to the existence of Buddha's own 'self' and that of others. The fact that Buddha used 'I' and 'You' is completely at odds with his 'soulless or selfless' doctrine. Secondly, the so-called Nirvana must first reveal itself to the soul in order to create enthusiasm in people for the journey that involves a search, comparison, acceptance and fulfillment. The soul is the immaterial tasting tool of the human being that distinguishes pain from relief. So, the reality or unreality of anything is discovered by the soul through the mind, and tested, compared, evaluated through the heart and chosen through the will— again with the involvement of the soul. You think with your soul, you decide with your soul, you evaluate with your soul. So in the whole philosophy of life, the soul plays a major role.

9. Why wouldn't you recommend Zoroastrianism and Islam to people?

In Zoroastrianism Satan is all-powerful. Therefore, neither God nor people are able to overcome Satan. In Islam, Allah has corrupted humankind and therefore they are not able to overcome the greatness of this corruption. In addition, Allah takes the righteous (if any) first to hell and then to paradise only if their good deeds outweigh their bad deeds. What Allah has done is unjust and illogical.

10. What would put Christianity above all other religions?

All major religions, besides Christianity, assert that evil has its origin in God or is created by God. In eastern religions, evil is part of God. In Islam, evil is created by Allah (Q.7:14). Whereas, the Bible states:

> *Holy, holy, holy, is Jehovah of Hosts; the whole earth full of His glory* (Isaiah 6:3).

> *God is light, and in Him is no darkness at all* (1 John 1:5).
>
> And then, anyone who follows the Holy God is holy:
>
> *If the root* (God) *is holy, also the branches* (God's followers) (Romans 11:16b).

Therefore, an understanding of world religions should certainly encourage people to believe in the pure God of Christianity.

The impurity of a god is frightening and gives people unlimited pain and suffering. Who is foolish enough to want unlimited suffering? In addition, religions that are the product of impure gods are not real and therefore cannot call upon people to be pure and righteous. How can an unrighteous god call upon people to be righteous? People, who are interested in the truth, never trust unrighteous gods and never desire unlimited pain and suffering.

11. How would it be possible to distinguish the true God from false gods?

A true God is holy and just, cannot have fellowship with sin, cannot create sin, is against sin and rescues people from sin.

12. Can people save themselves? Can a person's good deeds save him?

No-one cannot become their own savior. A prisoner has no power to release himself from prison. In the same way, humanity is in bondage to sin and Satan. Only the true God, who is over Satan, can overcome Satan and release people from their bondage.

There is no pure good in anyone's life, which would lead him or her to salvation. If there were pure good in a person's life he would no longer need salvation. People are impure, and impurity cannot lead to purity and perfection.

13. Which religion offers a pure heaven (paradise) to humankind?

The concluding section will clearly illustrate why only Christianity offers pure heaven to people.

14. What is God's plan for the salvation of humankind?

God is holy, just and love. He cannot remain indifferent to the injustice of Satan in human life. After the fall, God revealed Himself in His fullness (with His full capacity and characteristics) for saving people and restoring them to their original state of peace and happiness with God.

15. What does it mean that "God has revealed Himself (entered the world) with His full capacity" in order to save people? What is the motivation behind this revelation?

God loves the world and does not ignore the cry of men and women for salvation. For this reason, He has fully revealed Himself and is fully capable of saving anyone who wants to be saved. The Gospel of Christ says;

> *I* (Jesus) *have come that they* (my followers) *may have life, and that they may have it more abundantly* (John 10:10b).
>
> *For in Him* (Jesus) *dwells all the fullness of the Godhead bodily; and you* (the follower of Christ) *are complete* (free) *in Him, who is the head of all principality and power* (Colossians 2:9-10).

God is omnipresent. His full capacity is present in His act of creation and in His act of salvation for humanity. This is the salvation that the gods in all other religions not only are not able to provide, but also are not expected to provide. As we discussed earlier, they themselves are the cause of humankind's fall: because of their own dualistic nature they do not have freedom in their own nature and therefore are unable to free people.

A real God, more than a parent, makes Himself fully available, in all dimensions of life, in order not only to save His people (children) but also to make them victorious over the cause of the fall, as Paul, the Apostle of Christ said, to make them "more than conquerors":

> *Yet in all these things we more than conquerors through Him* (God) *who loved us.* (Romans 8:37)

God revealed Himself (in Christ) to Paul not only to save him, but also to make him victorious over Satan, destroying Satan's goals and purposes in his heart and mind. That's why he says we are more than conquerors.

Once, our thoughts, speech and behavior were bondage under Satan. We were cut off from the power, love and peace of God. But now, not only are we released from the dominion of Satan but we are also given authority over Satan through Christ.

By being empowered by the love of God, we can drive Satan out of other's lives. God not only saved us through His full revelation, but has also empowered us to demolish the work of Satan in other's lives. This is another reason why we are called "more than conquerors".

16. Why do we need the salvation of God for life on earth as well as life after death?

Salvation on earth means eternal reconciliation with God, which enables us to have a peaceful and loving relationship with other people, even from other nations. In other words, biblical salvation is the establishment of a right relationship with God and with fellow human beings on this earth and throughout eternity. When we say that, "We are saved", it means that immoral, unethical and hostile behavior—prompted by Satan—does not rule our lives anymore. This is what mankind needs in their relationships with each other.

14

Is the True God Just?

Ought not God to be Just?
Ought not People encounter God's Justice?
Where will People encounter God's justice?

The true God is just. He cannot tolerate injustice nor have partnership with it. In His creation, He has created everything, small or big, and put them in an orderly relationship according to His justice. Without justice things could not exist or co-exist in an orderly and peaceful manner; all would be chaos.

For the Creator, a normal and healthy family, or society, or world is a community in which every member fulfills his or her own role in a just or fair way with others. Without justice, humans live as strangers. Injustice bars people from knowledge, understanding and friendship and makes them ignorant, uncooperative (even hostile) and unfriendly toward each other.

God has created humankind in such a way that they yearn for justice. Even the cruelest person in the world does not like to be treated unjustly. So everybody wants justice. Thus, God would be inferior to His creation if He were powerless to achieve justice. If God as the ultimate reality is not just, why should human beings be just or yearn for justice? Why should one not breach the others' rights? God is the most high, and demands justice.

Those religions that do not view God as a pure being or that attribute evil to Him cannot be called religions of justice. Evil is contrary to justice. God is not the enemy of justice; He is it's enforcer.

Problems, Questions & Answers

1. Where should a person encounter God's justice, in this world, in the after world, or in both?

Justice must be applied to every dimension of life. All other religions except Christianity believe that a person must face and deal with God's judgment for his actions only after death. They do not believe that people must establish an eternal relationship with God in this life on earth. In other words, they believe that people cannot be purified and justified in this life. However, in Christianity, a person can experience God's presence and justice on earth even though evil and temptation exist.

As the ultimate authority of justice, God must establish His justice in the world for three reasons. First people need to have a peaceful relationship with God and others. Second, people must be instantly accountable for their own wrong doings. Third, God loves to enable people to act justly rather than waiting for a terrible punishment on the Day of Judgment for not acting justly.

A just God does everything that is necessary in order to awaken people to the importance of justice and to pave the way for them to live under justice as soon as possible. From a practical standpoint, we should never want to postpone justice until the future. For example, when a child does something wrong, the parents do not leave disciplining the child for years later, rather, they deal with it instantly so that the child grows in its understanding of fair play and the family can survive in and through justice.

Without the justice of God, life on earth would be anarchic and terrifying. The only religion that establishes the heavenly court of justice in the hearts of people on earth is Christianity. People have broken the law in their relationship with God and with others and are under the guilt of condemnation. For this reason they need to encounter the freeing justice of God in this world. The Gospel of Christ says;

> *And you, being dead in your sins and the uncircumcision of your flesh, He* (**God**) *has made alive together with Him, having forgiven you all trespasses, blotting out the handwriting of ordinances that was against us, which was contrary to us, and has taken it out of the way, nailing it to the cross.* ***Having stripped rulers and authorities*** (spiritual forces of evil c.f. Ephesians 6:12), *He made a show of them publicly, triumphing over them in it* (**Cross**) (Colossians 2:13-15).

> *For this purpose* ***the Son of God was revealed****, that He might* ***undo the works of the Devil*** (1 John 3:8b).

> *But it is now having been manifested by the appearing of our Savior* ***Jesus*** *Christ, who* ***has made death of no effect****, bringing life and immortality to light through the gospel* (2 Timothy 1:10).

> ***Salvation has appeared to all men*** (Titus 2:11).

> *Christ has made us free* (Galatians 5:1).

> *We know that we have passed from death to life* (1 John 3:14).

God's justice saves people from the bondage of Satan, sin and lawlessness in this present life on earth. Hallelujah! This is evidence of God's love towards the inhabitants of the earth, to preserve their lives through salvation in Christ, having made peace with God and made it possible to have peace with one another.

Evangelistic Conversations

PART IV

Each of these three evangelistic conversations is the result of conversations with many people. To be useful to the reader, they are summarized as a dialogue between two individuals.

15

Conversing with a Communist

Christian: Are you a good communist?

Communist: I believe so.

Christian: Now, you are living in a capitalist country and calling yourself a good communist. A North Korean also lives in a communist country and calls himself a good communist. Which one, you or the Korean, is the best between the two?

Communist: It depends on circumstances.

Christian: Exactly. That's why I said that Korea is living in the midst of a proletariat community and is close to the next revolutionary phase of a communist society, whereas you are living in a society that is run by capitalism and is far behind the advanced society of Korea.

Communist: Oh, no, no, no. I am living in a capitalist society, but I am not influenced by it.

Christian: First of all, you and capitalism are the product of evolution. Since you do not have any choice in evolution, how can you say that you are not influenced by capitalism? Secondly, you are a teacher and teaching in a school ruled under the so-called evils of the bourgeoisie, and thereby receiving the same salary the capitalist minded teachers are receiving and having the same capitalist benefits. How then can you say that you are not influenced by capitalism?

Communist: Well, my mind is communist and I spend my salary as a communist.

Christian: What do you do with your money?

Communist: I give some of it to communist friends who struggle financially.

Christian: Do you have a chance to ignore your friends and spend the whole money for yourself?

Communist: Yes I do.

Christian: How can you use your free will, since, according to communism, you are the product of economic forces and cannot have freedom?

Communist: Well, perhaps I am exercising freedom here.

Christian: You are using your free will which is denied in the evolutionary process. Don't you believe that stripping people of their free will is a sign of inconsistency within communist theory?

Communist: I need to think about this.

Christian: You admitted that you are exercising freedom and are not the by-product of an evolutionary process. Obviously, you are free to agree or disagree with me. Therefore, since you are exercising your own mind and free will to reject or accept something, you can no longer be a communist.

Christian: Let us continue our conversation from a different angle. Do you believe that there is or was a bad communist?

Communist: Yes, I would consider Stalin a bad communist because he killed many sincere communists.

Christian: How can you call someone sincere if there is no code of ethics in evolutionary communism? Or, how can you say that

Stalin was a bad communist since everything is based on the evolution of matter? Would not everything be considered good in its own time according to communist philosophy? Wasn't the era of Stalin—as the ultimate authority—the result of a dialectical war between thesis and anti-thesis? If he was naturally supposed to be there how can you call him bad? Because he has survived after the dialectical war between thesis and anti-thesis, therefore his presence, as Synthesis, and his actions must be accepted both evolutionary and revolutionary according to the framework of communist ethical codes; as a communist you are expected to reason within the parameters of your belief system.

In reality it was not a dialectical war that caused the tragedy of Stalin; it was his arrogance and self-will that drove him to deny the free expression of thought, to build the concentration camps and to murder millions.

Communist: Well, there were some people who were fighting for equal opportunity, but Stalin killed them.

Christian: I really do believe that people should have equal opportunities and be able to exercise their freedom. However, your comments about equal opportunity do not agree with communist theory that democracy is evil. Without democracy there are no equal opportunities. The respect for the rights of individual is so critical to a democracy. Stalin was against democracy because of communism and therefore he killed those who were fighting for equal opportunity and equal rights.

Communist: Yes, he killed many.

Christian: What is causing you, as a communist, to hate many people in this country since you call yourself a model of revolution for others? Have you never heard that the Bible, which is embraced by the majority people in this country, encourages them to love and respect others but not to hate? Do you not believe that there must be a difference between hate and love?

Communist: That commandment is useless since there are various classes in this country, and some exploit the others. We see many classes in this country from the poorest to the wealthiest ones. It is the capitalist Christians who have oppressed poor people and created an unjust situation in the society. Therefore, those whose rights have been disregarded have a right to fight against the wealthy—the oppressors—and even steal from them. God and his commands are outdated now. They are not relative; they are ancient history. The working class must fight and establish up-to-date moral laws and values.

Christian: I would invite you to consider how egalitarian are all the commandments of God: there are ten. In summary, all of them say that love your God with all your being, and love and respect your fellow men and women as you expect them to love and respect you. When God says love others and care for them as much as you love and care for yourself, it means that the law of God is not given to mankind to exploit or create difficulties but rather to make him/her responsible to stand against every evil thought, word and action. So, when you see injustice in the society, it is not from God or from his real followers but from those who are separated from Him, disregard His moral orders and therefore live against His will. God is good and every revelation and order from Him is good. He created humankind and designed a perfect plan for people. His plan and standard are against any kind of exploitation. Communism, humanism and all other man-made philosophies follow random life and therefore do not have a perfect standard (or a perfect ground) for mankind to live accordingly. The evolutionary mind-set has always left people in an imperfect situation, asking them to surrender themselves to a random life with capricious moral values. Isn't it more beneficial to follow a perfect standard rather than an immature one? From the depth of our hearts, all of us desire to have a perfect model in and for life. When our children are born, we love to provide every good opportunity for them so that they grow in a perfect environment. This is what God has done for humankind. Unfortunately, mankind has gone far away from God, lacks the necessary knowledge and therefore is in the state of loss.

There is a difference between the God of the Bible and the picture you have from God in your mind. In the same way, there is a difference between the real followers of Christ and many of those who call themselves Christians. God is holy and just and His moral values are against hatred, exploitation and injustice of a person against others. They are sins and against the nature of God, and mankind are asked to stay away from them through spiritual unity with God. This unity, on the other hand, gives way to respect, freedom of right, religion, belief and speech.

On the contrary, communism (Marxist-Leninist) encourages the battle between thesis and antithesis and sees hatred as an inseparable part of proletariat life. When do you think the communist society will rid itself from this hatred? You may say, "After the final communism takes place." Doesn't this worry you really that hatred will remain in the world, maybe billions of years, until the ultimate communism takes place? Don't you worry about your children to grow under the influence of this unceasing hatred? Don't you worry that this hatred accompanying communism eternally? Don't you think the instruction of the Gospel of Christ is great when it says, "hate is sin" and encourages Christians not to hate? Isn't it nice when a follower of Christ bases his heart on the original and absolute values of God and avoids such an eternal hatred and war of communism?

Communist: If this is your belief, I really appreciate it. But it seems to be unrealistic since there are no examples of this goodness in human history.

Christian: History is full of such examples and there are examples from our own contemporary times. For example, you are free to practice communism in this country because of these biblical values. Where are Christians free to practice their faith in communist countries? Can you imagine Christians rising up and saying "let us get rid of all non-Christians?" They do not have such a right from the scriptures.

This is one of the biggest differences between Christians and Communists. Christians have an ultimate standard for their belief and behavior that is based on a God who is the absolute standard of Justice, Love and Peace. He has revealed his perfect knowledge, his infinite wisdom and his righteous law through which the Christian blessed for loving his fellowmen and condemned for oppressing him.

I would like to give you a powerful and joyful reason for having God to rule our lives rather than human beings or matter. But to express myself in an understandable way, allow me to ask this question from you first: Would you like your child to grow up in a perfect environment or in an imperfect one?

Communist: In a perfect environment, of course.

Christian: You see! Even the way you respond is not communistic. Do people have free will to choose in communism? No. You desire to have a perfect environment for you and your child even though this personal desire does not make sense in communism. The reason I asked this question was to help you to define your life practically rather than theoretically.

To have an absolute standard for living your life is the most perfect method of directing your life. It means that your life—unlike communism—begins with a perfect method (you are created by a perfect God), is directed perfectly and ends perfectly. In communism, humanity is created by imperfect matter. How can imperfection lead to perfection? God, who is perfect, has created us and the world in which we live.

Since we are created by the perfect One, living with Him and are guided by Him, we have an opportunity to be transformed and be loving, respectful and peaceful like Christ. But those who begin with imperfect matter and principles will end with imperfect relationships even harmful ones.

Evolutionists leave people in a thoughtless and aimless environment for millions of years without any reason. God never desires people to be out of their minds for a second since

He has created them with intelligence. For this reason, thinking, planning, aiming and reasoning are precious to God.

Christian: Do you love your children more than my children or mine more than yours?

Communist: Mine.

Christian: According to communism, they are not your children and the children of your family. They are the children of evolution and of the social industry of the society. You are all a tool or channel of the economy—producers only. You do not have the right to claim ownership or any special right in relationship with your children or your partner. Therefore, when a communist says, "These are my children and I love them," it does not make sense according to the communist philosophy. And for this reason, under a communist (or socialist) regime, the state can take your children away from you at anytime or for any reason. If you complain or cry or feel pain, you are not a true communist.

Result of Conversation

My conversation with this communist continued for a few more months. One day, he openly questioned communism by saying, "I now can see a light beyond the physical world. What is this? I don't know yet. Maybe it is your God. Give me some time to think about it." Following his comments, I gave him a Gospel.

16

Corresponding with a New Ager

A letter from B.J.

Dear Daniel,

I heard your testimony in the website. I am sorry that you have gone through many difficulties. However, I believe that you have come out from one difficulty and put yourself in another difficult situation since Christianity is not the only solution. Christianity is also wasting people's life, pushing them to rely on a God who is not part of them and they are not part of him. If someone is not part of you how can he understand you and be united with you?

In addition, the God of the Bible calls you a measurable sinner who does not have any goodness in him to contribute towards the well-being of society. In contrast, the New Age gives our real identity to us in order to be able to use our full capacity for peace and unity. We have divine power, which is the source of every truth in us. Our personal meditations and experiences, therefore, are the products of this truth that leads us to the ultimate truth, and to genuine unity and peace. Since we are God and part of the truth, we are therefore free from limiting forces of churches and the stranger God of the

Bible and do not need their approvals for our personal feelings and experiences.

The reason for many problems in our societies is because people do not know that they have the light in them for their steps and future. Once they discover this treasure, they will enjoy their lives and become the real agent for the salvation of the world. Anytime I get in touch with the godhood in me, I am more peaceful, loving and blessing. I have all these qualities; what is left for me to borrow from outside? There cannot be any external reality other than I am. I am and have everything within me. I need to discover my fullness for leading myself to a better place. New Agers have authority to lead the world to painlessness.

Many people are brainwashed to believe in a God that does not exist outside them. No God or authority exists outside me. I am God and I have absolute freedom to use my own divine capacity for establishing my own ethical principles and be the light for my own life. Why should I limit myself to somebody else's principles since I have more and am able to discover the superior code of conducts in me? I do not need Jesus. He was just like you and me. Like me, he also discovered that he was God, and meditated on his godhood and led his steps to higher positions. For this reason, I wrote to let you know that I was also involved with church activities before. But then I discovered that church was a road-block to me to reach enlightenment. I quitted that limited life and now am following the real light. I want to encourage you that you need to rely on your own full power rather than limiting yourself to the nothingness of the church which says you are nothing in comparison to Jesus. You are God like Jesus and like him you can discover your deity too and even reach a position above him.

I hope you will make time to read this and reply. Thank you so much for your time. B.J.

Response

Dear B. J.,

Thank you so much for writing to me. I am grateful that I have received your email and words concerning your beliefs as well as mine. I am responding because of your interest in dialogue. I am sure you agree that ignorance and a lack of experience can cause many unpleasant things in families and societies. As you have heard and understood my story, you know that I have come to this place in my life through many up and downs. If I had known from the beginning, and if ideological authoritarianism had not blocked my understanding of truth, I would not have been exposed to so many dangers. For this reason, I am encouraged when I meet people like you who desire to share ideas. I pray our dialogue will be enlightening, helping us to understand the depth, width and height of truth.

Here are my responses to your comments. You said that as a follower of the New Age, you do not need the approval of others for your spiritual experiences since you are God and the source of all truth. In reality and in a very practical way this cannot be true for the following reasons:

Culture is the Product of Many

You need of others as much as others need you. Just as the members of a body need each other, so do the members of a society. The thoughts, words and works of a person influence the other members of his community. Since, we are communal beings we are influenced by each others' promises, inventions, music, food, poetry, infidelities, forces, etc. in a family or a community. These aspects of community compel us to openness, investigation, evaluation, decision making, approval, or sometimes to violation and whole lot of other things that the kinds of relationships in that community necessitate. The reason you wrote to me is that you do not want me to influence society in my way but rather adapt myself to your way of life and influence people through a journey in the New Age. I want to say to you that even your words are saying to me that you want to influence others or that you need others. You claim to be an independent, self-sufficient individual, but your words and actions prove the opposite. This is the danger of New Age philosophy, a kind of mysticism that closes the ear of its followers to the cry of others in the name of self-godhood, self-centeredness or self-sufficiency but in the mean time expects non-New Agers to listen to its calls! This is contrary to the philosophy of Jesus who believes that we are the members of one body and only through a mutual responsibility we can have unity or lead to unity.

External Influences Shape Us All

The second problem is when you believe that you are God and the source of all truth and therefore do not need the knowledge nor the approval of others. If this is the case, then your own personal feelings and experiences become the ruling forces of your life rather than the ultimate truth that is available to everyone and instructs all. Your own life journey that has brought you to this stage in your life is the proof of many external influences. You said that the LIMITING CHURCH LIFE caused you to search for a light. In other words, you were under the influence of church no matter for good or bad. Therefore, you will not be left alone to take your life journey to completion. You alone were not able to achieve your dreams and for this reason you needed to gain knowledge and mature your thoughts through your daily relationship with others. You went to school, learnt from others' experiences and since then you have been influenced and been influencing others throughout your life up until now. Without participation in a community life you wouldn't be able to learn perseverance. Also, in every step of your life you have gained the approval of your family's, schools' and country's principles, otherwise you should have been in prison now. Since the beginning of your live, you have been taught not to trust your feelings and experiences over the ruling principles of your family and society. As a member of a community, you need the knowledge and approval of others for your words, works, decisions and actions in order to live a normal life in that community. For example, if you did not pass your exams at the university, you would not be granted a diploma. If someone wanted to sell you a defective car you would not want to purchase it, since you have knowledge of other and better options. So, we always get help from external sources. How about if a flood takes us and we cry for help in order to draw people's attention to come and rescue us? No individual in the world has all the solutions for all of his or her needs and therefore is not the ultimate source for everything and hence, not God.

Society's Laws are Made by a Society

In a society, it is the law (external authority) of that society that categorizes our attitudes and behaviors as right and wrong. For example, it is illegal to cross the street when the traffic light is red. If a policeman catches you, he will fine you. Can you imagine a New Age Policeman saying to you, "*Just wait a minute, let me get in touch with my godhood and receive a divine revelation on how to deal with your driving problem and then I'll let you know.*" Such a police cannot exist in any part of the world, since every community needs law and order, and all individuals need to be treated equally. So, it is not every individual's personal experiences that regulate a society, but laws that are sovereign above all. Social relationships cannot be determined by an individual's desires or feelings, otherwise, life in that society would be anarchic. Therefore, law, order and ethical standards are not bound to one individual's experiences and decisions. Imagine someone in your family—one of your own siblings—comes to you after a meditation and says to you and your parents that he has heard an inner voice saying to him that he should kill you as a sacrifice. Would that be acceptable? Yet, similar things are still happening in India by individuals who believe that they are God and have authority to establish moral codes.

You Contradict Your Own Claims

You are criticizing Christians into believing in a God that exists outside them. Doesn't your belief (New Age) say that everything is right and good? Doesn't this mean that even those who do not believe that they are God and therefore are not in contact with their so-called inner divine power are good and acceptable? You see that not only your criticism is self-contradictory, your own conscience is also acting against your belief since you are criticizing. Your belief has said that you should not complain since everything is acceptable, but you are still complaining. This demonstrates that our dissatisfaction, anger, happiness, joy, patience, and conversation are all part of a great reality: we must live in a community by the principles of that community to be a part of that community.

Sometimes You Act Differently From Your Thoughts

You yourself avoid your own feeling or inner call and go against it. How many times have you said to yourself, "*I should do this rather than that*?" Often we sense that the achievements of others were better than ours; our desires or our experiences are premature or less profitable or even evil sometimes if we compare them with the desires and experiences of others. Also, we may desire beautiful things in our hearts, but as a result of the interferences of others we may end up with something very different from what we desired. Our hearts (thoughts and desires) may also lead us to pursue an unrealistic life. Therefore, there are other people around us and we need to evaluate our individual experiences and behaviors in the context of community's codes of conduct in order to survive. So, the inner voices and urgings are not always motivated by our own inner self but by the outside world as well. For this reason, we need a standard of comparison in order to listen and to discern the real and authentic voice and call. Once we are ready to accept such a standard in the context of the world around us, we may then be able to understand the superior values of Jesus Christ's call, which are truly amazing:

Who is more loving than Jesus?

Who is more just than Him?

Who is purer than Him?

Who knows more than Him?

Whose light is more than His?

Who is able more than Him?

And so on.

You believe that you are God and your life is run by your new feelings and experiences. This points to the existence of contradictions in your belief:

If God is the source of every good thing, then there is nothing left for him to experience or possess. Every good thing that you could imagine, God already possesses. If you are attempting to possess something you do not presently have, then you are not the God but a god of your own imagination. If you lack some aspect of truth, you cannot be the source of truth. It is inconsistent to say that you have everything in you but that you need to discover these things. If you haven't discovered them yet, how do you know that they exist in you? This is nothing other than a hallucination.

Also, the conflicting differences among people demonstrate that they are not God (who is self-existent, perfect and immutable) but are limited beings who need absolute principles to make their coexistence possible. Conflicting characteristics in individuals create different moral codes that can clash and create chaos if individuality becomes the base of a community. You know that in many ways you are different even from your brothers or sisters in your own family. If your brothers and sisters do not follow the rules in your family, but rather follow their own individual whims, your family will become chaotic. The problem is exacerbated if we follow our own individual preferences in a nation-state or in a globalized world. Imagine a situation where everybody becomes his/her own law-maker in a community with millions of people. Instead of having one law, the community will follow millions of laws. But alas, this is the very kind of society the New Age is trying to establish universal peace and unity? Are people more likely to have peace with a unified, sovereign law or with millions of different and conflicting laws? Would it not be better for you to give up your own limited godhood and principles and follow the principles of a sovereign God who is perfect and whose truth-claims are immutable? You and I are imperfect. Only a perfect Sovereign can lead us to perfection.

Does God exist outside of you or not? The New Age believes that God is universal (He is in everything, is everything and everything is in him) and impersonal. "God" is an impersonal "It." First of all, an impersonal god cannot exist. However, even if we could imagine that he exists, he, as an impersonal being, is external to you as a personal being. So, you see the New Age philosophy is saying, albeit indirectly, that God exists as an external and independent being. Since your philosophy insinuates that God is as an external being, you should not blame others for claiming the same thing. However, there is a real reason for the existence of sovereign God who is in control of everything and distinct from His creatures. Every created thing shows that it has a cause (Creator) and a reason for its existence. When you create a pen, you are not a pen but the creator of that pen with a purpose. In other words, you are outside of that pen, and its creator; the pen is the pen of your image created for a specific purpose. In the same way, God exists separate from us and created us in His own image for a distinct purpose.

God exists. He is perfect. He has perfect plan and purpose for the lives of individuals and communities.

Have you ever thought deeply about what you wrote saying that, "*Anytime I get in touch with the godhood in me, I am more peaceful, loving and blessing.*"? I know that this is what New Agers believe, but this again refers to another contradiction inside the philosophy of the New Age:

This means that when you are not in touch with your godhood, you will not be peaceful but hostile, not loving but hateful, not blessing but cursing. According to your belief where everything is the same and there is no difference between good and evil; why then are you trying to focus on your meditation for good?

Second, why do you still feel obligated to get in touch with your godhood since the outcome of your relationship or lack of relationship with it is the same?

Third, why should people forsake their beliefs and follow New Age beliefs if their new status after conversion is no different from their previous status?

Fourth, for the above reason, no criticism of any idea matches your philosophy since everything is good for you. Therefore, your concern for me that I have been wasting my life with Christianity do not make sense.

As a result, a Christians' life and relationship with God—the Creator of the whole universe – is logical and satisfying compared to your so-called internal-divine-relationship:

In the New Age, you say that you do not need others and that you are not accountable to others since you are the source of your own truth and values. Christians, believe that God is the source of absolute truth and that they can trust God to guide them to the truth and enable them to live in the truth. Accordingly, every Christian is responsible for his/her words and actions in their relationships with others.

For Christians, God is a personal God and, therefore, people can have a personal relationship with Him. People and God can have a personal relationship with each other.

Christians who have a relationship with God eschew evil, because God is good. Good and evil cannot have a relationship.

God is the absolute source of Truth, Justice, Love and Peace—people are not. This makes God superior to humankind; it makes Him Lord. This lordship over His creatures is logical since He is the source of absolute truth, justice and love and is superior to the relative truth, justice and love of mankind. As Christians we believe that if we enthrone God in our hearts and pursue His truth, we will have a better hope of obtaining our goals.

The experiences of millions of mutable men and women cannot be taken as a foundation for ethical principles; right and wrong are individualistic according to New Agers and they evolve with new experiences, feelings and discoveries of each individual person. But the values of an immutable God are always the same and are therefore, superior. Hence, it is practical, logical and easier to follow an infinite God than it is to follow millions of finite men and women who differ from one another, who change continuously and who are not immune to making mistakes.

Christians have an absolute standard to determine right from wrong. Every word and deed must be measured by an absolute standard in order for the world to be rational and practical.

It is gratifying to know that I am not God—that others are not God. As fallible human beings we have all experienced pains and we all have caused pain to others and have broken their hearts. If we were God, all of our heart-breaking words and deeds would have become the creeds of a religion of human weakness, and would have caused pain forever.

As regards Jesus, Who is He? What did He think of Himself? He did not discover late in His life that He was God; He was always conscious of His divinity—a divinity from eternity past. Before Jesus was born, the Old Testament scriptures spoke of His divinity and of His humanity nearly three hundred times. The Prophet Isaiah, who lived seven hundred years before Jesus, called Jesus:

> "*Wonderful Counselor, Mighty God, Everlasting Father, Prince of Peace. Of the increase of his government and peace there will be not end. He will reign … forever*" (Isaiah 9:6-7).

In His life on earth, Jesus did things that only God could do. His miraculous birth was unique. His unconditional love for sinners is inexplicable; His sacrifice for others is unmatched; His resurrection and ascension to heaven are unparalleled. These supernatural qualities of His life on earth were given to prove the divinity, the eternity of His existence.

Personally, I am convinced that Jesus is the Mighty God for the following reasons:

The Bible says that there is One God and One Creator for the universe. I knew this already, but I did not know that the Creator of the universe had to be personal in order to be able to create, because creation requires the revelation of God in order to touch, create and sustain. Impersonal God cannot touch, create and sustain any personal being (i.e. us) since his (its) own nature is untouchable. This logic is also true for salvation. The personal God of the Bible revealed Himself to save us personal beings. Therefore, if creation necessitates God's revelation, so does salvation. God revealed Himself in Jesus to save the world.

Why did God reveal Himself? Because:

God is love. If you have a beloved in your life, you will understand what I mean. The nature of love is to bring the love and beloved ones together in unity. Love motivates you to protect your beloved one and to express your love to him/her. Love makes your relationship romantic and your attitudes cool, attractive and meaningful. Love causes you to sacrifice yourself for your beloved one if necessary. In the same way, when God is the object of your love, you need to throw yourself fully into the ocean of His love in order to build your identity in Him, otherwise, you will be distracted by other relative loves, which are here today and gone tomorrow. When you throw yourself into this love, then all your thoughts, words and deeds will be in love, and you will be able to apply the qualities of your lover in your relationship with others:

> Love your lover, God, with all your heart, mind and soul,
>
> Love your neighbor as you love yourself,
>
> Love your enemy, because love overcomes every unloving thought, word and action,
>
> Love your spouse as you love your own body.

We can see that God revealed Himself in Jesus in order to teach us the height, depth and width of this love. Obviously, everyone would benefit if each one would immerse them self in this love?

God is just. Every just society requires an absolute standard of justice and a perfect administrator of justice to achieve their goal. God is that standard and He is that administrator. Yet you (New Agers) claim that you—that everyone—is a god, therefore there is no need for courts, governments, prisons, wars, and family problems need not exist. I say, that if we are gods, we are certainly useless gods because all these unsolved problems abound among us; not only we, humankind, haven't been able to solve them, but we have been making the world a more unsafe place than ever before. Why? Because in making ourselves gods, we have ruled the true God out of our lives. There are no solid principles that relate mankind to one another anymore, especially among the western communities. Our individualism has become so predominant that it is difficult for us to come out of our personal zone and sacrifice for others. Whatever, therefore, we do to put humanity at the center of our belief and practice we only add more to our existing problems.

We must recognize that there are powers in us and in our surroundings that are holding us from useful improvements. God is able to help us to overcome the obstacles. If we follow his standards in every aspect of our lives and in the lives of our families, our societies and in the world, we will find ourselves becoming good children, good citizens and good employers or employees. No organization in the world is run without a standard, a plan, a goal for achieving the standard and the channels that take it to the set standard. No family, business and society can randomly reach a set standard. If we ignore even a little part of the set standard, we will not be able to reach to our desired standard. It is the same with the authority of a sovereign God. He has salutary values for every dimension of our lives. If we ignore His absolute values and rather follow our relative values and principles, we will not be able to treat each other equally. In addition, our millions of individual principles will clash with each other and create chaos. If we allow God into our lives, our relative principles will be replaced by the absolute and beautiful principles of God.

God is Savior. We need to be saved from our self-centered rules and be put under the sovereign rule of God. Otherwise, every one of us will hurt others. If we put ourselves at the centre of everything, then we will justify every pain or disaster caused by us. For example, if a person rapes our child, he simply can say to us that it was his inner truth or godhood that led him to do so and therefore there is nothing wrong with his action. You can see that if every person is granted such a right his personal feelings and experiences become the basis for his actions. But if we invoke a public law that denies the "right" of arbitrary rape, then everybody is protected. By accepting the authority of such a community law, we say "no" to our individual "rights." This is the same with God and the law of His territory. God is the giver of life and has perfect principles for life. For this reason, we ask Him to renew our minds and hearts in a way that we can live justly and treat others equally based on His unconditional love. In such an environment we will be able to have a peaceful family, community and world. When we abide in a perfect God, our plans will be perfect and led perfectly. We are imperfect; by our own power we are not able to lead our imperfect life to perfection. Logically speaking, imperfection cannot lead to perfection, but perfection (God of the Bible) can lead imperfection (humanity) to perfection. Isn't it safer to be led by the perfect God rather than by an imperfect human being? By saving us, God changes our identity from imperfection to perfection. Here is another great difference between the biblical and the New Age philosophies. The emphasis in the Bible is on "Being" first, but in the New Age is on "Doing" first. In God, you have to BE enabled and taught first for doing perfect things, but in the New Age you, as an imperfect being, are asked to DO randomly for reaching to perfection. If you are not changed and put in a perfect environment, you will not be able to receive perfection no matter how eager you might be. This is the simple and logical philosophy in Christianity; you have to be saved first and then do, which is the opposite of what the New Age (and other religions) believe—you have to do in order to save yourself. If we are not saved and haven't become the citizens of God's Kingdom of peace, love and justice how can we keep His principles and have peaceful and loving relationship with others? We need to allow our identity to be renewed first or be established on the solid foundation of peace, love and justice in order to be able to have good relationship with others. For this, we need to allow the sovereign God, as the Perfect Commander of life, to enter our hearts and lead us according to His principles of life. Salvation from God is more trustworthy than salvation from people. The salvation of God, as the perfect and good role model, makes us loving, peaceful, humble, broken, repentant and grateful towards God and our fellow men and women. So, God revealed Himself to save us.

God is helper. God with His love and justice rescues us from the threats of our self-centered ambitions and from the external obstacles, and situates us under His leadership and principles. After that, He always makes Himself available to help us for living our new lives. He helps us through His presence, power and providential guidance, thought His infallible word and through the encouragements of others. But this help attends only those who have believed in the salvation provided by the grace of God and through the death, burial and resurrection of Jesus Christ. God is very practical in His approach to humankind. He works in the context of real life. If we rescue someone from a flood or fire, we also try to provide something for him to survive. Certainly, God would not do less. Nay, but His provision for those He saves is greater and His heart is more loving than mere men. Also, He has the best instruction for us to avoid our own selfish "floods" or to those dangers external to ourselves.

I hope this answers your words. Please respond; I will be so delighted to continue the conversation with you.

17

Dialoguing with a Muslim

Ali Invites Me to Return to Islam

I listened to your testimony. Your criticism of Islam was really unrealistic. Islam is the greatest religion in the world, with over one billion followers. How could you say Allah is not the same God Christians believe in? Allah's glory is manifested everywhere in the world! I love Allah! He is my fountain of life and my savior! He instructs me on how to pray and live daily. Without Him nothing exists. With Allah I can do everything. He has sent Muhammad, the best man in the history of men, so that we can follow his example and receive Allah's mercy.

Why would you leave the merciful Allah and join a religion that is older than Islam? Judaism is the preliminary step in religion, Christianity is the second, but Islam is the final and perfect step that Allah has put ahead of us so that it can take us to paradise. Many Christians have been coming to Islam in order to receive the final revelation and blessings of Allah, but you have left Islam and gone back to a lesser step. Islam is the civilized and perfect way that answers every question of life and can become a light for your steps. Your sins will be forgiven if you put yourself under the umbrella of Allah and follow Muhammad. His promises for paradise are also other celestial rewards that will make your heart joyful. Do not allow the wrath of Allah to come upon you; throw yourself into Islam's arms and join over a billion Muslims in the world.

Evaluation and Reply

Comments on Ali's Words

Ali's elegant words about Allah, such as glory, fountain of life, savior, merciful, and about Islam, like civilized and perfect religion, may be attractive to a person who does not know Islam, but not to me. Obviously, he does not know his religion in a broader sense and for this reason he is using words that do not make sense in Islam. Muslims have been using such words for centuries in order to keep Islam alive without knowing that these words do not make sense according to the nature of Allah. As soon as Ali learns that Islam does not have anything to offer him, his unrealistic joy will start to wither.

Praise the one true God (*"To you it was shown, that you might know that the Lord is God; there is no other besides Him."* Deuteronomy 4:35) that I am prepared for such a confrontation and could not be enticed by his statement. I can be more than a mere guardian of my faith by troubling myself to answer Ali's statement and take this conversation to a new level, possibly one that will prove to be life changing for Ali. As the experiences have proven, I can anticipate the result of our conversations if I can hold Ali interested in continuing the conversation. With this in mind, I would aim to respond to him in such a way that would keep him both interested in the conversation and constrained to answer my questions.

Generally and experientially speaking, having once been a Muslim myself, when Muslims are not able to answer a question, the tendency is to immediately change the conversation and raise other issues. This is the most difficult part of keeping a conversation alive with them. This can prove to be challenging, but with a little patience one can encourage the nature of the conversation to stay on track and to move forward, step-by-step. As in any conversation, it is key to consider whatever point the other person is trying to make. However the overriding focus must be on the main issues that can get his conscience and his mind engaged in a fruitful conversation and to discover the nature of Allah in comparison with the God of the Bible. My first question to Ali would be: "*Is Allah really the fountain of life and giver of joy?*" I would be careful to ask this question in a way that is not aggressive or confrontational. Aspire to always draw others with the loving attributes of our God.

So, it is key to focus my questioning on exactly the root of Ali's beliefs or there will be no challenge to keep his interest, nor will there be any opportunity for a deeper consideration on his part. I must prove, through gentle biblical reasoning that Allah is in fact **not** the fountain of life and joy, but an imposter. Only then will I be able to break through the illusion that clouds his mind, and provoke him to seek the True and Living God for himself.

Normally, Muslims evangelize not because of their knowledge about Allah and Islam, but for different reasons:

They were told that Islam is the best and perfect religion, and they have accepted it without having knowledge in comparison with other religions and beliefs.

They have great reverence for God and want to please Him and gain rewards for their future.

Their salvation, even though uncertain, is based on their good deeds; evangelism is a good deed too.

All of these reasons, and certainly many others, compel Muslims to get involved in religious activities. They hope to enter heaven with religious activities. We, as the followers of Christ, do not enter heaven by our activities, but by our identity (spiritual citizenship) in Christ. In Islam and in all other religions, "Doing" is the most important thing for entering heaven, but in Christ "Being" comes first. They "do" (or rely on their own works) in the house of sinful Adam, hoping to enter the sinless house of God (heaven) in the future (though even this is uncertain) but we "are" already transferred into this house (the Kingdom of

God), are citizens of heaven and act because of salvation not for salvation.

Muslims do not understand that righteousness is not obtained by following a sinful man (Muhammad) or in the house or belief of a sinful man, but in the house of the righteous God. Muslims do not understand that first and foremost, they need to be transferred from the sinful house of Adam into the pure heavenly realm in order to have a good environment for doing good. Before entering into the house of God (being saved), how can a person be good in the house of sin since every good thing belongs to heaven? Is there any good thing outside of God that a Muslim can put his trust in or on which he can base his actions? No, there is not. Every good thing, including salvation, freedom and peace, comes from above. That's why we need to surrender ourselves to the Prince of heaven first before attempting to do good works. This is what Jesus teaches. He is the way, the truth and the life that bridges and connects us with the one true God (and Heaven) (John 14:6). To follow Christ into His Eternal Kingdom we need only surrender ourselves into His gentle, loving and saving hands. What religion can boast of such a gracious and loving God, who made His own provision so that we would be *guaranteed* eternity with our Savior! Perhaps that is the only question one needs to ask a dying world filled with self-righteous corpses!

I must pray for Ali's courage to continue our conversation, to overcome the fear of Islam, and also that God would humble him and deal with his heart in such a way that he would answer the questions truthfully. Courage is always needed to accept the gospel as well as to present it. And there are times when more grace is needed, especially now when I would purpose to target the very root of Islam and dig much deeper into Ali's logical thinking.

Reply to Ali

Thank you so much for your writing and responding. I am sure that you agree with me that obedience to an idea or a religion must involve understanding, comparison, evaluation and eventually decision-making with confidence. For this reason, I need to raise some fundamental questions about your comments and I need to get an honest response so that we both will be able to have a productive conversation which will lead one of us to leave his belief and follow the belief of the other. These are my questions:

Do you agree with me that God must be kind, merciful, just and loving in order to become the source of life and joy for people?

Do you believe a kind, merciful, just and loving God would create calamity for the soul of people or inspire people to sin?

Would you agree that a God, who creates calamity or sin, cannot be a source of life and joy for people?

Comments on Questions

The reason I asked these questions from Ali is because the Quran says that Allah is the creator of all disasters from eternity and it is he who has corrupted Satan and inspired sin in human beings. If this is the case, then Allah cannot be the source of life and joy. At this stage, I did not want to mention anything from the Quran directly, because I needed to get his response based on his conscience first. Then, step-by-step, I will show him that logically the words of Allah (the Quran) are not historical and do not even relate to human life.

Ali's First Response

I absolutely believe that God (Allah) is kind, merciful, just and loving. In fact, he has 99 attributes that describe His nature. If you listen to your conscience you will be able to discover how merciful, fair, and caring God is. Our consciences are in fact universal and linked to God; it is in this way that we get the peace and joy of God. God has given us the blessing of using our intellectual capabilities to decide which way to choose. He has given us the only true path, Islam; we need only to follow His path.

Another source for the joy of our soul is God's divine words, the Quran, which is true and has never been altered. The Qur'an teaches how to perfect oneself in order to achieve peace, happiness and success in this world and be elevated to God's paradise in the life after. The Quran has rules and regulations about how to live in the community and build your relationship with people and ultimately how to worship God. The revelations of the Quran are also scientific and it is amazing that the Messenger of God (Muhammad, peace be upon him) knew these things while he was unlettered.

We Muslims believe in destiny. This means whatever happens to us is because of Allah's desire and there is a reason and wisdom for it, which is always to our benefit. He created good, bad, disaster, sin and the devil. He guides whom He wishes and leads astray whom He wills.

Evaluation and Reply

Comments on Ali's Words

Any time Muslims mentions Muhammad's name, they also say (peace be upon him). This is because Muhammad was not sure about his future, therefore Muslims think that he may be under pressure and for this reason they ask Allah to give him peace.

Ali has almost answered all my questions. His response has raised issues very relevant to our discussion, and has interjected some errors that must be dealt with.

What are his errant ideas and why has he raised them?

> *The Quran has never been altered.*

He said this because Muslims believe that the Bible is changed and cannot be trusted anymore. Somewhere in our conversation, I need to challenge him to rely on his god-given intellectual capacity to compare between the Quran and the Bible and see that his claim is nothing but a baseless propaganda. I also need to help him to understand that both the Quran and Hadiths (Islamic Traditions) directly confirm that the Quran was changed, but there is no evidence in the Bible nor in the history of Christianity that the Bible has been changed.

Also, Ali said:

> *The Qur'an teaches how to perfect oneself in order to achieve peace, happiness and success in this world and be elevated to God's paradise in the life after.*

Ali does not understand what he is talking about. The Quran says that people are sinners and imperfect. Ali needs to understand that he (as an imperfect being) cannot lead himself to perfection. This is a good apologetic issue for discussion. I will bring it into our dialogue every time I will find an opportunity.

He also speaks about peace. Is there any place for peace in Islam between Muslims and non-Muslims? Is he aware that happiness and success in Islam are not spiritual and godly, but worldly and at the cost of non-Muslims' loss? However, I have to try my best and avoid conversing with Ali about these things because he means more political and social peace, happiness and success rather than spiritual and these may lead him to turn our conversation into an argument. I need to avoid argument (2 Timothy 2:23-26).

Also, Ali said:

> *The Quran has rules and regulations about how to live in the community and build your relationship with people and ultimately how to worship God.*

My goal is to lead him to Christ and release him from these rules and regulations. Closer to his salvation, he will understand that these rules and regulations will not be able to save him. Also, he will be shocked to understand how harsh, cruel and humiliating these rules and regulations are to women, to moderate Muslims and to non-Muslims. Presently, I must avoid talking about them in order to help him to find the true way of building a relationship with God. For this, he needs to understand who the true God is, how can we have personal relationship with God (receiving Jesus as the "Son of God") and be saved.

Also, Ali said:

> *The revelations of the Quran are also scientific and it is amazing that the Messenger of God (Muhammad, peace be upon him) knew these things while he was unlettered.*

Islam is a political religion and therefore very predisposed to exaggeration. Muslims use words like 'scientific' or 'unlettered Muhammad' in order to attract people's attention to themselves. First of all, Islam's own references show that Muhammad was able to read and write. He may have not been proficient in writing and reading, but he was able to read and write. Second, he was a tradesman for years, travelling from Mecca to Medina and Syria, and heard and learned many things from the surroundings and later reflected on some of them in the Quran, now known as the science in Islam. One scientific thing that Muhammad attributed to himself was when 'he was able to cut the Moon in half,' referring to the position of the Moon when its half part is seen in the sky. Muslims believe that it was Muhammad who split the Moon into half.

However, my goal is not to prove whether or not the Quran is scientific, but whether it can reconcile Ali to God and to people. This is an urgent spiritual thing for him to know.

The relevant words in his response to my questions are:

God is kind, merciful, just, fair and loving

God has put a conscience in us so that we can use our hearts and minds and refer to our consciences for decision making

Nothing happens without the permission of God

God is the creator of all disasters, sins and he leads astray; everything is from God.

Can a just, holy and loving God create sin? He said "Yes", whereas the real response must be "No". It is here that I need to get his mind to working, and his conscience activated in order to turn him away from a god (Allah) who is the creator of sin and disaster.

Reply to Ali

You have agreed with me that God must be merciful, loving, just and fair. This is great. However, in your response to me you also said that God is the creator of the Devil, all disasters and sins. Don't you think that a merciful, just and loving God should not and cannot corrupt the Devil or create disaster and sin?

Let me express myself through a couple of examples:

Example one: Let's suppose that you are a kind and just father who sincerely loves his child:

As a merciful, loving, just and fair father would you willingly create a disaster for your child?

Do you train (or prepare) your child to do evil to others or would you get an evil person to harm your child?

Do you inspire sin in your child or prepare him in a way so that he can act as an unrighteous or a lawless person?

I cannot imagine that you would want to do any of the above to your child. Therefore, if you, as a limited human being, do not desire such things for your child, how then could a God who is called the source of justice, holiness and love desire such evil things for humanity?

Example two: In our societies we have law-makers who make laws in order to protect the rights of people. In addition to their good services, do any of them have also the right to prepare gangsters (devils) in order to break the law and threaten the rights of people or to cause other disasters for citizens?

If law-makers—the defenders of human rights—are against any evil actions and eschew creating problems, why is your god (Allah) not able to refrain from creating sin (a disaster for soul) and to restrain the devil whose goal is to destroy peace? The real, holy, just and loving God cannot create sin for the destruction of the human soul. For this reason, it is irrational and also blasphemy to attribute the creation of evil and sin to the God of the Bible. Creating sin is immoral and a sin itself; God cannot be immoral since He calls himself the holy God.

On the other hand, a god who creates sin does not have the right to ask people to avoid sin and to act righteously. By creating sin he himself has acted unrighteous. How then he can call on others to act righteous since he himself has acted unrighteously? Therefore, a god who corrupts and creates sin cannot be fair in his approach to people. The followers of such a god also cannot be fair in their lives and relationships with others. How would you avoid sin and lawlessness if your god was not able to do so?" No matter how much you hate sin and unrighteousness, you will always act unrighteously if such a god is your spiritual leader.

In reality, a god who creates sin and corrupts people as well as the Devil, does not exist. A god like this is the product of a man who created his god in his own mind and in his own image.

Here is the great difference between the God of the Bible and the Allah of the Quran:

The God of the Bible has not corrupted the Devil and has not created sin and disaster for the soul of mankind

Allah has corrupted the Devil and created sin and disaster for mankind

Since you mentioned that we need to rely on our consciences to make a good choice, doesn't the God of the Bible seem more authentic to you? My conscience is saying to me that only the God who does not create sin can be trustworthy but not the one (Allah) who has created sin. In the same way, a father or a mother who protects his/her child from disasters is more trustworthy than the one who becomes a threat to his/her child. Isn't this true? What do you think?

Ali's Second Response

God is mighty, self sufficient and merciful. He does not need any help from any one. He is not like His creatures that need to eat or sleep. He is perfect and unique in every way.

Well, are you sure that the Gospel is 100% authentic and that it is the actual revelation to the Prophet Isa (Jesus)? Has the Bible not been distorted and altered over time?

And did you know that the Qur'an has never been altered and distorted because God has promised that no one can change His words? But the Bible is changed. In the Old Testament you were not allowed to eat pork, but now you eat it. You were allowed to have more than one wife in the Old Testament, but in the New Testament you cannot have more than one wife. Also, you call Jesus God whereas he has clearly said that he was not. Like every one, he ate, slept and was in need of everything. God is not in need of anything. Jesus did not die; nobody could kill such a great prophet. He is not dead, he is alive and in heaven. He will come in the last day in order to confirm the truthfulness of Islam.

It is clear that Christians and Jews have removed these facts from the Bible, and for this reason, the present Bible cannot be trusted. If the rebellious people did not change it, it would be similar to what the Quran is. How can the words of the Bible be different from the words of the Quran since the Quran is the last holy book given to humankind through Muhammad who is the seal of prophets? Don't you think that prophets must call people to the same faith?

However, you said that the God of the Bible has not corrupted the Devil. If this is the case, then where does sin come from?

Of course that is a valid thought that God should not have created sin but everything happens by God for a good reason. He is able to create sin and able to destroy it too. He is Just, Loving and Merciful.

I hope this answers your questions.

Evaluation and Reply

Comments on Ali's Words

Ali has sensed the power of my logical approach to him. He has realized the truth in my response to him and for this reason he said, "*Of course that is a valid thought that God should not have created sin.*" However, his Islamic pride has not allowed him to confirm this but instead has rushed him to justify the unethical works of Allah.

Praise God that one response has opened his eyes this much so far. I need to pray much for him now and I also need to encourage him to stay on track rather than beating around the bush. The best conversation is when it starts from the root and intelligibly leads to the branches step by step. In this case, I need to help him to understand who Allah is first, and then open his eyes to the political, social and moral values (branches) of Allah in comparison with the values of Christ. But this is not what Ali is aiming to do. He is trying to change the subject for his own convenience and to eventually escape the conversation simply because he is not able or does not want to answer the questions. I need to get him to answer my questions fully and to understand that we are not communicating only for the sake of conversation but for clarity. I need to help him to realize that he started the conversation and he needs to stay on the subject and answer my questions.

It is obvious that he has enough logical power to confirm my discoveries about his god, but because of Islamic pressures he is hesitant. One of these pressures is that Islam must always be the winner. Therefore, it is not easy for Muslims to say "Yes" to any other thing that Islam does not confirm even though it is true. It will be costly for them if they hold something else above the words of Muhammad and Islam. For this reason, they feel safer if they change the subject (or lie) and release themselves from the pressures and punishments of Islam even at the cost of the truth. So many of them are terrified to compare Islam with other religions. It is easier for them to speak irrationally against other religions rather than to question Islam or to put their life at risk. For this reason, Ali has raised the issues that are commonly used by Muslim evangelists for the falsification of the Bible's message. So, my task will not be easy; I must get him to stay on track and speak the truth. I will be persistent in this.

Ali has tried to raise the following controversial things in order to change the subject and rescue himself:

- The Bible was distorted and altered over time and therefore it cannot be trusted.
- The Quran is unchangeable and contains the genuine words of God
- Jesus was not God but a man who ate, slept and was in need. He was not killed, but taken to heaven without experiencing death.

If I comment on these issues, he will not be able to understand my responses simply because he has not completed his homework for the first step yet. He needs to know first whether or not his god, Allah, exists or if he is good. If he does not exist and is not good, then his words will not be good nor trustworthy. If Allah has created sin with his own hands and has authored the Quran with those same hands, how can the Quran be trusted? How could Allah create sin unless the essence of sin existed in his own nature and image. In other words, only a sinful being can create sin. If this is the case, then this means sin is eternal in Islam since Allah is introduced as eternal. If sin is eternal, this means that sin is infinite in Islam. (Muslims also believe that Allah is infinite and eternal). Can there be two infinite beings? No. If both sin and Allah are infinite in Islam, this means sin and Allah are one. In other words, Allah is sin, and sin is Allah. By introducing such an image of his god, Muhammad drove his religion and doctrine into chaos. Apparently, he borrowed from contemporary paganism that believed sin was created by God. If Ali understands the chaotic nature of the doctrine of Islam, he may put away the Quran and Allah and release himself from the thoughts of Muhammad and open himself to the Spirit of God.

After discovering the attributes of the true God, he will be able to distinguish the truthfulness of the Bible against the Quran and may allow the Spirit of God to plant His words in his heart. Then, he will be able to judge rightly between Muhammad and the prophets of the Bible. He is misinformed by Muslim scholars and evangelists, and I need to help him to understand the truth.

There are some issues in his response that can help us to continue the conversation and challenge him more. I am going to let him know that my goal in raising questions is to help us to compare our religious presuppositions in relation to God. So they are important and he needs to answer them.

Reply to Ali

Well, I was expecting you to answer directly to my questions raised from your comments. You rather have raised issues that are irrelevant to our discussion at this stage and have also started judging Christians' belief according to the Quran. You were going to rely on your 'god-given intellectual capacity' in order to evaluate the beliefs rather than relying on Muslim scholars' prejudices. We need to first discover whether or not Allah or the God of the Bible is real and then discuss the accuracy or inaccuracy of the Quran or the Bible. So, our first step is to know who the author of the Quran is. If we discover that Allah cannot be the true God, then his book, the Quran, also cannot be authentic. The same step is also applied to the God in the Bible or all other gods in all other religions. Therefore, please answer my previous questions and allow us to move ahead step by step.

However, I found an encouraging comment in your response, "*Of course that is a valid thought that God should not have created sin*". I am glad that you have sensed that it is invalid when the hands of the ultimate law maker (God) of the universe are involved in creating sin and putting peoples' life in risk. It was discouraging that just following this comment you have tried to justify the invalid work of Allah by saying, "*but everything happens for a reason that is His divine knowledge.*" No wisdom can justify a holy God—who must hate sin—to create sin. Actually, God's divine knowledge cannot be a reason for Him to create sin; it is a reason for Him to eschew sin. When you say, "divine," you indicate holiness, righteousness, godliness, majesty, beauty, perfection. Sin cannot be holy or beautiful or majestic. In the same way, the creator of sin cannot be holy or righteous or godly. So, let us always keep in mind that a holy God cannot create sin and must separate himself from sin. With this in mind, we have discovered the following differences between Christianity and Islam so far:

Christians are following a God who has not created sin

Muslims are following Allah who has created sin

Let us refer to our conscience now:

Is creating sin a sin in itself? Both, logic and conscience confirm that creating sin, and thinking, speaking and acting sinful are all sin. As a result, if Allah has created sin, he is a sinner.

Whom do you think we should follow as our spiritual role model? The creator of sin or the hater of sin? Should we encourage people to follow the God who separates Himself from sin or Allah who does not?

Both conscience and wisdom prove that "sin" is a problem. Therefore, it would be better to follow the One who is not a problem-maker, and that is the God of the Bible.

If we encourage people to follow Allah, then they have right to challenge us with the following questions:

What rights does Allah have to ask people to avoid sin (unbelief) since he himself brought sin into peoples' lives?

Why would Allah punish people for sins he himself has created? People are sinning because Allah has made them sinners.

Why does Allah punish people and send them to hell for the unbelief he himself has caused?

Logically, Allah is responsible for the sin he has brought into the world and he must be weighed in the balances of absolute justice himself. Conversely, the true God does not create people in turmoil, sin and lawlessness, and He does not judge them for someone else's lawlessness.

Obviously, sin makes people disloyal and disrespectful. Why has Allah tried to make people disloyal and disrespecting towards himself? If this is his decree, then he does not have the right to punish them when they ignore him.

In reality, sin prevents us from having a loving and intimate relationship with God. By creating sin, Allah has created a wall between himself and people and against intimate relationships. This is not what the true God does, and therefore Allah cannot be the true God. If he is not true, then his words (the Quran) cannot be true. In other words, if the root (Allah) is not holy, neither are its branches (the Quran, Muhammad, Islam, etc.). Muslim scholars seem to be ignorant of this obvious fact. Though Allah himself proves not to be the true God, these "scholars" are trying to prove that the Quran is truthful. For this reason, I began our conversation with Allah (the root of Islam) in the hope that you would be able to see the corruption in him, avoid him, his religion and his prophet. The real problem lies at the root of Islam, Allah, and Muslims are unaware of it.

Let us believe that God is holy and sinless who has made us for Himself so that we can have a loving and heavenly relationship with Him. He who is holy and sinless is able to be a good role model for us, wipe our sins away, take us to heaven and make us holy. Allah who is the creator of sin cannot be a good role model and is not able to lead us to heaven.

In the mean time, I would like you to understand that the Muslim Scholars' claim concerning the corruption of the Bible is baseless: they believe that both the Bible and the Quran were written in eternity by God, and that the original copies are preserved in heaven. They also believe that no one can change the words of God. On the one hand they say that "*no one can distort the word of God* (the Quran)" and on the other hand they say that the Bible (word of God) was distorted. Isn't this a contradiction? If you believe that the Bible was the word of God, given to guide Jews and Christians, how could any one distort it? Are you saying that God was not able to protect His words in ancient times but was able to protect it in Muhammad's time? Do you believe that God is the same yesterday, today and forever and is always able to protect His words? Muslim scholars have spread many baseless things about the Bible and Christianity and have left themselves vulnerable to the judgment of God, but you need to be careful since you are able to compare and discover the truth yourself.

Let us see how sin came into this world according to the Bible. Satan abused his free will and rebelled against God and his rebellion was the first sin that entered into the world. This is different to what Islam teaches. The Quran says that Allah corrupted Satan. You see how the Bible stands above the Quran in this matter too. The God of the Bible is holy and just; He cannot corrupt. Whatever the God of the Bible created from the beginning was good and beautiful. From the beginning "Satan" was not known by this deceiving name. His name was "Lucifer" and he was a good angel before the fall of Adam and Eve. Lucifer abused his status (he was an archangel with great authority), rebelled against God and fell from his godly position. For this reason, God called him Satan. Then Adam and Eve were deceived by him and fell from their holy estate as well. So, sin came into the world by man through Satan—not by God.

As a parent loves his children, God also loves mankind and unlike humans, He is the source of absolute love. He created mankind for Himself in order to live among them and demonstrate his glory. Sadly, humanity rebelled against God and went astray. Since God is all-loving, all-wise, all-knowing and all-powerful He has determined from time immemorial to redeem people from their sins and restore him to his original state. God loves to save men and women from sin. As we do not want our children to stay in dangerous places even for a second, so God feels the same way. Sin is horrible—tragic in God's eyes; it has created a wall between God and the creatures he loves. God wants to destroy that wall of separation and restore a healthy and happy relationship with mankind. The lack of salvation and uncertainty in human life is like a burden to God. That is why He determined to save mankind through His amazing revelation. The Quran is missing all of these wonderful expressions of the loving heart of God and of his divine initiatives for the salvation of mankind on this earth. The Bible teaches:

If sin has ravished people's lives here on earth and separated them from God, He has determined to redeem them from their sin and restore them to Himself.

God is mighty, holy, just and loving; he can save people here on this earth. Leaving the salvation for the afterlife alone means leaving mankind in toil and pain in this life. God loves people and He is ready to pay the price and save them from their sin and from Satan's captivity.

So far, we have discovered the following reasons for why the Bible is more trustworthy than the Quran:

The Bible teaches that a Holy God cannot create sin and that he does not make people faulty (sinful), while the Quran teaches that Allah made people sinners and faulty.

The Bible teaches that the God who hates sin and destroys the work of the devil (sin) is the best role model, but the Quran teaches that Allah, who is the creator of sin, is the best role model.

Evidently, Muslims believe that God was not able to protect His words (the Bible) in ancient times, but the Bible teaches that God is the same yesterday, today and forever and that He is always able to protect His words.

The Bible says, if you unite with God here on earth, your unity with God is eternal and you will pass the judgment in afterlife. But if you refuse the salvation God has provided, you will go to hell, and you will not pass the judgment in the Last Day.

Isn't it beautiful to receive the assurance of salvation (being with God) in this present life rather than dying in uncertainty? Deep in the heart of mankind there is a voice that is always crying for union with God. But, mankind's sin has erected a wall between them and God. If they are not cleansed from their sins, they cannot have communion with a holy God and serve Him. The service and worship of an unsaved sinner cannot approach a holy God. A person must be in union with God before he can serve Him. That's why the Bible teaches that cleansing from sin is the first step for being right with God and being able to serve Him. Only salvation brings you to God and unites you with Him. If you are not saved you are unable to be with God. For this reason, Muhammad was not able to teach confidence about his future to his followers. He died in uncertainty; he did not know what was going to happen to him after death. If he had been united with God on earth, he certainly would have been able to say where he was going after death, but he was not able to confess such a confidence because he was not saved. How can a person, who is not saved, lead others to salvation? It is impossible. Jesus is in heaven and for this reason he is able to lead us to heaven too. Every one of His followers is saved and has confidence about his relationship with God both now and forever.

Salvation and the confidence of being with God are the realities that must take place in this life on earth. Let me give you an example in order to make this more understandable. Imagine your child has run away from home. You are always crying and praying for him (or her) to come back. One day, he realizes that nothing and nobody is receptive as are his parents and family. He therefore returns back to home. You see that "going astray" and "coming back" are both the realities of the life on earth. However, when he comes back and knocks the door what will you do when he says to you, "Hi Dad, I have come back"? Do you welcome him in immediately, or do you treat him as Allah treats people? According to Allah you would say to your son, "I have to weigh your deeds first and see whether your good deeds outweigh your bad deeds, then I will be able to let you in." But this is not what a real parent does. As a parent, you will jump with joy, hug him and then bring him in immediately without questioning him about what he has done. This is the way the God of the Bible receives people. He receives them first in order to be able to change them afterward. For this reason, He is called Father. He opens the door to people who come back to him and changes (saves) them with his kindness so that they can fellowship with Him on earth and in heaven forever. God is a loving God. As you jump and hug your son with excitement, cry and say to your child, "Welcome back my darling, come in" the real God does the same. Isn't this an amazing difference between Islam and Christianity?

Allah asks a fallen person to save himself (or herself). How can a fallen person lift himself to the place where God is? How can a lost child get into his father's house unless the father opens the door and rescues him without accusation? Only God's power can save us, get us into His house (heaven) and allow us to be transformed in that house in order to be able to think, speak and act righteous like Him. If we are not saved by God and do not have an eternal relationship with Him, we will not be able to lead others to Him. Allah has left his followers in confusion and with an ambiguous religion—Islam—and therefore he, his religion and his followers are not able to point people to the real way (or path) to heaven.

The God of the Bible is not like Allah. He opens the door for sinners, cleanses them Himself so that they can be with Him both now and forever. God knows that a sinner (lost) cannot think, speak or act righteous when he (or she) is not saved. A sinner must be put into a sinless situation (or house) first and then he is able to act righteous.

In the Quran, not only is salvation left to life after death, but it is uncertain as well. Muslims are not sure whether or not God will forgive their sins and save them in the afterlife despite their hard work in this world. Every Muslim, including Muhammad, says, "Allaho Aalam" which means only God knows about their future. How can you call Islam the perfect religion, when it is unable to give you a perfect response about your standing with God both now and in the future? A follower of Christ is with God now and will be with Him forever; his (her) destiny with hell is canceled eternally. Please understand that when you call Allah mighty and all-knowing, this betrays the uncertainty Allah has left you with:

If Allah is mighty why then he is not able or does not want to save Muslims here on earth? Are his hands too short to save? While Satan is able to lead people astray from God in this life, is Allah unable to lift them up again in this life? If Allah is unable then he cannot be the real God.

Second, if Allah is all-knowing, why was he not able to give confidence of salvation to Muhammad—his best man—and to his followers for their future?

Third, if Muhammad did not know about his future, why would he put pressure on others to follow his uncertain footsteps? Why would people follow an uncertain person? Isn't it better to follow Jesus Christ who is in heaven and the source of our confidence rather than in Muhammad who expressed an overriding uncertainty?

Because of this confidence we follow Jesus. Your so-called distorted Bible is full of assurance compared to your so-called perfect Quran, which has left Muslims in uncertainty. If a religion is not able to give assurance to its followers, we should not follow it.

From the beginning we agreed that we need to rely on our consciences and the logical power God has given us in order to be able to compare and make the best choice. Every religion says that it is the only genuine and perfect religion in the world. It would be irresponsible if we simply believe claims without actively comparing them in all aspects. Doubtless there is only one God for the universe, and for this reason there must be only one Way (Path) to God. Therefore, only one religion can be true, not all. How can we discover the true one and distinguish it from the false ones? Only by reading their holy books and making a thorough comparison. If this be the case, then what are the criteria for a religion or belief to be false? It is when that religion attributes illogical, unholy and immoral things to God. The Quran attributes the creation of sin and corruption to God. The real God cannot act immoral and create sin or corrupt the Devil. If a god is involved in creating sin and takes a stand against the Truth, Justice, Holiness and Righteousness, that god is not real, but the product of the mind of a sinful man.

What do you think?

Ali's Third Response

In Islam there are many ways that you can purify yourself from sin. First of all, you need to convert to Islam. When you convert to Islam your past sins are wiped away and you are like a newborn baby. After that, anytime you sin and sincerely repent of your sins you will be forgiven.

You claim that if a person is not saved his worship will not be accepted by God, because he is living in sin and chained to the principles of Satan. If this is the case, how can you call God merciful? We Muslims do not worship God blindly because we are assured that we are on the right path. When we pray, fast, give alms or get involved in jihad we feel accepted by God.

God pardoned Adam and Eve due to their repentance to God. Muhammad is the same. God has already said to Muhammad that his past and future sins have been forgiven. He is the most pious, humble and eligible servant to enter heaven. In fact, he will enter the highest rank in heaven among all the other prophets and messengers. He is the best in character out of all mankind. If you listen to Muhammad, you will also dwell in Paradise. God elevates those who are obedient to him and receives them into heaven.

You said that you belong to heaven now. How can this be? There cannot be heaven on earth. Why would heaven include the sin and chaos of this world? But if you mean that you have peace of mind and that you are assured of heaven in the next life, then that is something we have in common.

You are right: God was not less careful in the past, but He is the same always. However, God has a plan and his plan is better than all our plans. He has already planned that the last messenger to mankind would be Muhammad (peace be upon him). Muhammad's name is mentioned in all religions' holy books. He was sent to finish the unfinished works of all other prophets. So, all other religious books are outdated now. Only the Quran is legitimate. However, all the past prophets and messengers are brothers in faith.

It would be impossible to find an authentic Bible these days because it was distorted many centuries ago and is probably wiped out and the Qur'an has revealed this fact. Forgive me for being blunt: why would you still follow the Bible, which is full of doubt and uncertainty, whereas the Qur'an has every answer for your soul? Why are you following a book that was written by men? Why not follow the Quran, the actual word of God? Everybody knows that the Bible has been altered. For proof of the Qur'an's authenticity, it has been pointed out by scholars that some of the scientific discoveries of recent times were mentioned by Muhammad—fourteen centuries ago—before there was any such thing as technology.

What does Jesus have to do with your sin? His deeds were only enough to save himself. Jesus cannot forgive on God's behalf and take his followers to heaven. Jesus is a slave of God like we are the slaves of God. No one has right to speak above God.

Evaluation and Reply

Comments on Ali's Words

Ali is confusing himself by bringing many issues from all mountains to a valley, mixing them together. His lack of knowledge has caused him to be trapped in the misinformation Muslim scholars have spread everywhere in order to dissuade their followers from reading the Bible or listening to Christians. I asked him to focus on the first step and respond to my questions, but he has refused to do so. He may do this again and again, but I will not give up and need to remind and encourage him to continually focus on the main issues. I believe this demonstrates that it is not that simple to lead a Muslims to Christ. You need to pray always and ask for the guidance of God and for His special touch.

From this time on, I need to ask him for Quranic references in support of his comments. Muslims say so many things that are not supported by Islam. Also, I need to communicate to him with references if possible. So far, I believe that I have raised all the necessary issues for him to understand the inaccuracy of his religion. I just need to remind him again and again through various ways and examples.

We saw in his comment that he believed that he could purify himself of his sins. He does not know that by practicing some religious ritual he will not be able to purify himself. Purity means freedom from the rule of Satan and coming under the rule of God. People in other religions are not able to grasp the fact that they need to be transferred by God from the kingdom of Satan into the Kingdom of God in order to be purified by the Spirit of God. Purification under the rule of Satan is impossible since Satan does not believe in purification and does not allow you to align yourself with God. There is no ground for purification in the kingdom of Satan. Paul put this in words like this:

> *Therefore, as through one man's offense judgment came to all men, resulting in condemnation, even so through one Man's righteous act the free gift came to all men, resulting in justification of life. For as by one man's disobedience many were made sinners, so also by one Man's obedience many will be made righteous… so that as sin reigned in death, even so grace might reign through righteousness to eternal life through Jesus Christ our Lord* (Romans 5:18,19,21).

Ali needs to understand:

If humankind's fall (unity with Satan) occurred in his life on earth, his salvation (unity with God) must take place in this life also.

A loving, caring and just God never leaves the salvation of people to the afterlife.

He said, "*Scientists are amazed how scientific Muhammad's messages were! Or the Qur'an has every answer for your soul.*" Like lying and deception, exaggeration also is part of Islamic doctrine of *Taqiya* (holy deception) and is used in evangelism too. Exaggeration is also used to frustrate opposing conversing parties and create deviation in conversations. Muhammad himself was the cause and originator of such exaggerations: he did this in order to receive psychological approval from his people,.

Judeo-Christian values were wide-spread in the Saudi Arabian Peninsula, and Christians and Jews were civilized groups of people and highly respected by Saudi Arabians. Muhammad said to his followers that his name was recorded in the Bible. After his death, his followers followed his footsteps and included other religions too.

Soon after Muhammad's death, his followers invaded the neighboring countries and established Islamic imperialism. In the following two centuries after the rise of Islam, Muslims gained access to education and read the Bible and were unable to find Muhammad's name in it, and concluded that the Bible was corrupted. They were not able to question the authenticity of the Quran—if they did they would be killed. So they claimed the Bible had been corrupted. There was no threat for degrading the Bible; they were highly praised for doing so.

I need to get Ali to rely on his God-given conscience and compare Islam with Christianity and the Quran with the Bible.

Reply to Ali

We agreed to use our consciences and logic in our discussions from the beginning. My aim in our conversation is not to win this conversation. I rather aim to bring the fundamental beliefs of Islam and Christianity to the surface so that we can discover which one is the best light for our steps. We are not here to impose our beliefs on one another either. To make a belief our own, we need to base our decision on knowledge and understanding; otherwise we become blind followers of that belief.

Also, we need to agree that we are accountable in the presence of the just God for every word we have been saying to one another. So, let us be sure that for every answer we give to one another God is also a witness to it. The just, holy and righteous God expects us to stand for the truth, rather than throwing unnecessary words into the discussion for the sake of saving ourselves from a simple confession. I don't want us to miss the point, which is 'Discovering the Truth Together'. You haven't answered my question on why you prefer to follow the creator of sin (Allah) rather than the God of the Bible who hates sin. It is hard for me to believe that your conscience accepts such a thing from Allah.

You need to ask yourself who is your role model in daily purification? Is it Allah? Allah has created sin and he cannot be a good role model of purification. Creating sin is sin itself. Sin militates against eternal assurance as well. Therefore, Allah who is the creator of sin cannot give you assurance. For this reason, it is wrong when you say, "*We are assured that we are on the right path*". The creator of sin cannot show you the right path; this is just a false notion that you have received. In the same way, Muhammad cannot be a good role model for you either. He died in uncertainty according to the Quran and Hadith. An uncertain person cannot show a certain path to you. The following passages of the Quran and Hadiths prove that Muhammad died in uncertainty without having any assurance about his future:

> *Say (O Muhammad): "I am not a new thing among the Messengers* ***nor do I know what will be done with me*** *or with you. I only follow that which is revealed to me, and I am but a plain warner"* (Q.46:9).
>
> *Narrated Abu Huraira: I heard* ***Allah's Apostle saying, "The good deeds of any person will not make him enter***

> ***Paradise."*** *(i.e., None can enter Paradise through his good deeds.) They (the Prophet's companions) said, 'Not even you, O Allah's Apostle?' He said, "Not even myself, unless Allah bestows His favor and mercy on me." So be moderate in your religious deeds and do the deeds that are within your ability: and none of you should wish for death, for if he is a good doer, he may increase his good deeds, and if he is an evil doer, he may repent to Allah."* (Hadith Bukhari 6: 70: 577).

… 'Aisha further said, "**And whoever tells you that the Prophet knows what is going to happen tomorrow, is a liar**." She then recited: **'No soul can know what it will earn tomorrow**.' (Q.31:34) … (Bukhari 6: 60: 378).

You are saying that the sins of everyone who embraces Islam are forgiven and he becomes like a new born baby. This is contrary to Islamic beliefs. If Muslims' sins are forgiven, why then was Muhammad—who is above everybody in Islam—not able to know whether or not he was going to heaven? We suppose that you become like a new born baby and start from the scratch after you become a Muslim. What is then causing you to sin again and become uncertain about your future while you have entered the purity of Islam? Why is the pure Islam not able to prepare you to stay purified, avoid sin and have confidence about your future? What is the benefit of being forgiven of your past sins but left unprotected from your future sins that undermine your confidence? It seems that Islam attempts to save people from one flood by dropping them into another. Isn't it good to follow Jesus who saves you once and for all?

There is no doubt that God is merciful to sinners, but only to those who ask Him to save them from sin. Adam and Eve were deceived by Satan and sinned against God. As a result they fell from their lofty position with God and were cast out with Satan. After they discovered that they had lost all the blessings of being with God, they cried to God and He accepted their repentance, covered their sin with a sacrifice, forgave them and lifted them up again to their previous spiritual position. This is what I want you to experience. Adam and Eve fell into sin during their life;

God saved them during their life and before they died physically and they proclaimed the assurance of that salvation. Understand that becoming separated from God because of our sin and rebellion and being redeemed by God's grace and restored to fellowship with Him are transactions that must take place in this present life—the afterlife is too late.

This is something which Islam does not admit and makes no provision for. It denies the possibility of reconciliation with God because it denies the only way God has decreed to redeem mankind from his sin—through the vicarious sacrifice of Jesus the Christ who takes away the sin of the world. If Satan is able to deceive people and destroy their relationship with God, then God is able to redeem them and to restore that relationship. Satan is not greater than God! How could a loving and just God refuse fallen humanity crying for salvation now? Do you lift your fallen child immediately, or do you leave him on ground for the life after?

You are saying that Allah is merciful to Muslim sinners only, but not to non-Muslims. Sin is sin no matter who does it—Muslim or non-Muslim. If Allah is merciful, then why does he tolerate the sins of Muslims but not the sins of non-Muslims? This is discrimination, not mercy. This is not what the Bible teaches. God loves sinners and is merciful to them, calling them to repentance and faith in the Lord Jesus Christ for the forgiveness of their sins. Jesus said: "*I am the Way, the Truth, and the Life; no one comes to the Father but by Me.*" (John 14:6)

A sinner, who is not saved and cleansed from his sins, will not be able to worship a holy God. God transfers sinners from the kingdom of Satan to His Kingdom first and then permits them to worship Him. Before your prayers, fasting and alms God wants your heart and your presence with Him. No matter how good a prodigal child may be in his life, his goodness will never satisfy the hearts of his parents until he is found and taken back to home. When he is in home, he will receive mercy and forgiveness. The best use of the mercy of God is to surrender to His rescue from sin and Satan. This is the difference between the

Bible and the Quran. The Bible says that God desires to forgive your sins in this present world, but the Quran says that Allah leaves your salvation until the afterlife without any promise of certainty.

Also, the real God does not call an unsaved person "righteous." Whatever a sinner does is mixed with sin. In the eyes of a holy God the best work of a sinful person is like a filthy rag (Isaiah 64:6). For this reason, God wants to clean the heart of person first. When God comes into your heart, He fills your heart with His presence and displaces Satan. After this, you will not be slave to sin anymore, but a slave to God and to his justice, holiness and love. So, you have to die to Satan first and be born in God again in your life on earth in order to receive His mercy and forgiveness. This is what the mission of Jesus Christ is. He came to regenerate people and release them from the bondage of sin and Satan.

Jesus is more powerful than Satan. If Satan was able to make people sinners and separate them from God, Jesus is more powerful to bring people back to their original state with God. God drove Adam and Eve from the Garden and from intimate fellowship with Himself because humanity yielded to Satan's temptation. God will draw people back into fellowship and blessing if they will yield themselves to Christ and to His triumphant death and resurrection. In other words, if Satan is able to make people unrighteous in this world, Jesus is mightier than Satan and able to make people righteous not only in this world, but in the world to come. If people could be separated from God in this present world, they can also be reunited to God in this present world. This is why I insist that to leave the work of salvation until after this present life (as Islam does) is an unwarranted tragedy.

If your child cries for you to rescue him from danger, you would not ignore his cry and tell him that you will rescue him later—perhaps after he dies. You would rather rush to his aid, risking your own life in order to save your child. Would God do less than a parent; would he be less caring? No. God is anxious for the salvation of sinful men and longs to save them as soon as possible.

Please tell me, what is wrong with being saved now, with being reconciled to God in this life on this earth rather than being put off until after this life with a dreadful uncertainty? Isn't it better to be saved by God earlier?

You said that Muhammad is the most pious man. The Quran says that Muhammad was a sinner in his entire life (Q.48:2). Interestingly, the Qur'an never attributes sin to Jesus. Why is Jesus not called the most pious since He has never sinned, yet Muhammad is called the most pious despite his past and future sins? Could you please tell me why you don't follow Jesus who is sinless and in heaven, yet you follow Muhammad, who was a sinner, died and was not able to ascend to heaven like Jesus did? What would God be most pleased with: following one who was sinless, or one who was a sinner? The holy, just, loving and fair God would never command us to turn away from the sinless One and follow a sinner. In God's view, the status of a sinless one is always greater than that of a sinner. For this reason, it is wise to follow the sinless One (Jesus) as our Role Model.

You also said that heaven cannot be experienced on earth. If this is your belief, then how can you experience righteousness and piety (you said that Muhammad was pious) which are the fruits of heaven? Secondly, God is everywhere. Wherever God goes, He carries His identity and values with Himself. His reign is on earth as it is in heaven. If God is near us, His Kingdom is also near us. Thirdly, the Kingdom of Heaven is spiritual. It is established in the heart. If Satan is spiritual and lives in the human heart, God is also Spirit and can live in the human heart. When God's kingdom is established in the human heart, the kingdom of Satan is destroyed. A person's heart becomes a paradise when God reigns in it: that heart is saved from captivity to sin and to Satan and it is delivered to be in the service of God. Hallelujah! God has determined to save souls on this earth and He does what He determines to do. That's why I am saying to you that I am saved, because He is in my heart and Satan does not have dominion in my heart anymore. My heart is the temple of God. And for this reason, I know that I belong to heaven now and forever. I am not uncertain or in doubt; Satan and Hell were cancelled by the work of Jesus Christ. Yes, Satan had separated me from God, but now through Jesus Christ I have been reunited with God. In Islam I did not have confidence (God) in my heart, but now by believing in Christ I have received that confidence (God). All the followers of Christ are assured of their future, but in Islam even Muhammad was not sure whether he would be able to enter heaven or be rejected.

There is even a more shocking statement in the Quran which says that all the righteous (including Muhammad) and the unrighteous will be gathered around hell first (Q.19:68-72). Then if anyone's good deeds outweigh his bad deeds, he will be taken to heaven. This can create serious questions in the mind of people concerning the doctrine of Allah, the Quran, Islam and Muhammad:

Why would Allah take his so-called most pious man and his righteous followers into hell first? Your so-called distorted Bible says that the righteous is like the apple of God's eyes and he belongs to heaven and will be taken to heaven directly.

How could Allah call Islam more perfect than Christianity since Islam takes righteous people through hell to heaven but Christianity directly?

Why would the so-called perfect religion, Islam, leave righteous men and women in an imperfect situation with uncertainty about their future?

If Muhammad was not assured how could you be assured abut your future?

Why Allah leaves his righteous followers in uncertainty? Isn't confidence better than the lack of confidence?

How can you say, "*We Muslims do not worship God blindly because we are assured that we are on the right path*"? Allah has left you without assurance about your future—your spiritual eyes are blind to your future. This means that you are following Allah blindly. How can you know you are on the right path?

Jesus came to the world 600 hundred years before Muhammad. He guaranteed heaven to His followers. His followers believe in Him because He is sinless, has ascended to heaven, saves sinners, and gives them assurance of their salvation. Muhammad lacks all these qualities of Jesus. The real God never sends a sinful man like Muhammad to finish the work of the sinless One, Jesus. It is the sinless One who is able to finish the work of God on earth. Therefore, Muhammad cannot be the seal of prophets, but the sinless Jesus can be. In the same way, the words and the book of the sinless One cannot be outdated. Whatever the sinless One thinks, speaks and acts is the reflection of God's very holiness, justice and love. Only Jesus is able to guide people to the Kingdom of Heaven. He is alive and in heaven and is completing the work of God on earth in a perfect way, but Muhammad who is a sinner and dead cannot finish the work of God; he cannot do anything.

You agreed with me that God is always careful and watchful of His words. Then your claim concerning the distortion of the Bible is contradictory. Simply to rely on others' prejudices does not help you to discover the authenticity of a book, a religion or a person. You need to listen, compare and discover for yourself.

The following is a summary table of our conversation (and also a few other differences) which all together may help you understand that your so-called distorted Bible stands far above the so-called unchanged Quran. The Truth speaks for itself. We need to open our hearts and minds to the Truth and avoid justifying things that are not true:

The Bible says	**The Quran says**
God is holy and cannot create sin.	Allah is the creator of sin and disasters, and the best of deceivers.

The Bible says	The Quran says
You must be saved here in order to have peace with God and people.	You may be saved after life.
Jesus is sinless. The sinless can do the work of God perfectly on earth and is a good role-model.	Muhammad is sinner. A sinner cannot do the work of God perfectly and be a good role-model for others!
You have assurance of salvation	You do not have assurance of salvation
You have freedom of choice in order to choose your faith. Freedom is from God and He respects peoples' freedom.	No body can leave Islam, otherwise they must be killed.
You should not lie to anyone.	Muslims can lie for the sake of Allah and Islam.
God revealed Himself to Adam and Eve and many others.	God did not reveal Himself to Muhammad.
Jesus said: love non-Christians and pray for them.	Muhammad said: kill non-Muslims, curse them and do not become friends with them.
Jesus said that the real love is between one husband and one wife.	Muhammad said that a Muslim man can have four wives and use slave girls.
All people are the same in the eyes of God. No one is better than the other one. Because all are sinners.	Non-Muslims are unclean (najis), dogs, pigs, donkeys, monkeys and worst of beasts. Only Muslims are good (though sinners).

The Bible says	The Quran says
Love everybody unconditionally. Love creates peace.	Do not become friends even with your father and brother if they do not practice Islam as they are expected.
Husband must love his wife as he loves his own body	Husband can beat his wife

How can you say that the Bible with these qualities is inferior or outdated? Do you still call the Quran unique in comparison with the Bible after seeing all these?

Based on the realities we have to compare, judge between the two books and discover the one that contains the words of the real God. People may say to you, "Even if the Quran was true, I wouldn't want to follow it and call others animals or beat our wives; we'd be better off to follow the Muslims' so-called changed and corrupted Bible, which stands for equal opportunity and introduces the sinless Jesus as the Role Model for life".

If we have agreed to base our conversations on logic and conscience and confirm the authenticity of everything by reference, then there is no need for you to jump into a conclusion and say that the Bible is distorted or the Quran is the only genuine book. You rather need to read or listen first, compare the scriptures and their teachings. Afterward, present your conclusions and decision with solid reasons. Otherwise, the conversation will not be fruitful.

Christians have never believed that the Bible was changed, whereas Muhammad himself, his successors and Muslim scholars as well believe that the Quran was changed. Please consider the following:

Did you know that the Quran, the Hadiths and the Sira of Muhammad all confirm that many Quranic verses were changed by Muhammad and even the present Quran is not the perfect one in comparison with the other seven Qurans Othman, the third Kaliph (Khalifah), burned?

Muhammad believed that some later verses of the Quran were better than the former verses and he therefore changed them himself:

He cancelled (Q.2:106), took away what were revealed (Q.13:39; 17:86), and changed one verse for another (Q.16:101). For example, Muhammad prayed towards Jerusalem for about fifteen years, and then changed the direction towards Mecca simply because Jews did not follow him and he turned his face from Jerusalem, the Jewish religious city, to Mecca (Hadith Bukhari 1: 2: 39).

Classical scholars argued that anyone who studied the Qur'an without having mastered the doctrine of abrogation (cancelation) would be "deficient" (Abu al-Kasim Hibat-Allah Ibn Salama, *An-Nasikh wal-Mansukh* (Cairo: Dar al-Ma'arif, 1966), pp. 4-5, 123. On pp. 142-3, he lists the abrogated verses. See also pp. 7, 11, 26-7, 37, 46). So you are called to believe that the Quran is changed.

Because of this, Muhammad was actually accused by his own countrymen for forging or inventing verses (Q.16:101; 32:3).

Even Satan inspired verses in Muhammad (Q.53: 19-20; cf. 22:51-52), and this put a question mark on Muslims' claim of the sovereignty of Allah and the immunity of his Quran.

Even the Quran confirms directly that it was turned into shreds:

> *And say: "I am indeed he that warns openly and without ambiguity,"—(Of just such wrath) as We sent down on those who divided (Scripture into arbitrary parts),—(So also on such) as have made Qur'an into shreds (as they please). Therefore, by the Lord, We will, of a surety, call them to account, For all their deeds* (Q.15:89-93).

All the alteration above is against the following claim of Allah:

> *The word of thy Lord doth find its fulfillment in truth and in justice: None can change His words: for He is the one who hears and knows all* (Q.6.115).

Muslim scholars are still studying the alterations of the Quran. Did you know that when you put the various translations of the Quran side by side that they do no match each other in many places and in the numbering of verses? How can human agents translate the words of Allah differently or change it?

Do you know that the Sira of Muhammad (his biography) narrates on how Satan inspired the first revelation (the first chapter of the Quran) to him (Ibn Hisham, *Sirat Rasul Allah,* P.106-107)? Do you know that once Muhammad asked his followers to prostrate in front of the idols Al-Lot, Al-Manat and Al-Uzzah according to a verse in the Quran, but this verse was taken out of the Quran after the death of Muhammad? (This verse is still preserved in the Islamic ancient commentaries and traditions.)

I mention these few examples for you to understand that even Islamic books and Muslim scholars confirm that the Quran was changed by Muhammad himself and by those who had memorized it. There were eight versions of the Quran and no one, not even Muhammad, was able to distinguish the true one from the false ones. This created tension among Muslims after the death of Muhammad and Othman had no choice but to burn the other seven and keep the present one. These evidences are all in the Islamic books and are confirmed by Muslim scholars.

It is shocking that with these clear evidences you do not call the Quran distorted but rather call the Bible distorted even though there are no Christian or Jewish evidences for any possible change? Every logical person must expect the book of Allah, the Quran, to be distorted, since Allah himself started his mission with corrupting the soul of mankind. A corrupter corrupts everything, including his own words. For this reason, I preferred our conversation to begin with the knowledge of Allah so that you could see that the corruption in Islam began with Allah and had permeated all else in Islam.

Ali, I am glad to say that I am grateful that you are able to take advantage of the Judeo-Christian freedom of speech in a non-Islamic country even to say that the Bible is corrupted. Freedom of speech and of religion is valued in the Bible. In contrast, the Quran says to kill those who criticize the Quran, or Allah, or Muhammad. Because of Jesus, you and I are able to converse freely in a non-Islamic country. We wouldn't be able to do this in any Islamic country in the world. Isn't the freedom of religion and speech and the equal opportunity in Jesus Christ nice?

Ali's Fourth Response

I must confess that some of the issues you have raised have taken me deep into thinking. I may need to go back and read our conversations from the beginning again. I have started to enjoy our conversations.

However, what do you mean by sin? Is it our daily transgressions or something else? Also, you said that only a true follower of Christ can worship God. Why?

For years I have based my heart on the following Islamic beliefs:

> *Belief in the One God*
>
> *Belief in angels*
>
> *Belief in God's revelations i.e. Torah, Psalms, the Gospel of Jesus and the Quran.*
>
> *Belief in the prophets of God*
>
> *Belief in the Judgment Day*
>
> *Belief in Al Qadar (the good or bad that Allah has ordained for us)*
>
> *I have always believed these things since they are clear beliefs. We also have religious obligations and instructions in Islam which guide us to be more submitted and obedient to God compared to you Christians who do not have any set daily prayers:*

> *We witness that Allah is the only One God and Muhammad is His messenger.*
>
> *We pray five times a day, in before sunrise, midday, afternoon, sunset and night.*
>
> *We fast in the month of Ramadan.*
>
> *We give alms.*
>
> *We also have pilgrimage to Mecca, only obligatory for those who can afford.*

Aren't these practices helpful in protecting Muslims from sin or to purify them?

Also, Muslims wash themselves before prayers, but you Christians do not wash for prayer. How then you can pray to the holy God since you are not clean?

Allah has promised a beautiful future to those who do good and avoid evil. He will show mercy to us if our good deeds outweigh our bad deeds. Why shouldn't we believe that his way is the perfect way? How about a true Muslim who repents with sincerity and fights against sin; do you believe that he still falls short of entering paradise?

It is wonderful to be saved here in this life on earth but it is difficult for me to understand on how Jesus saves since he is a man and needs salvation himself. Also, your belief in 'three gods' (the trinity) and calling Jesus the "son of God" add to the difficulties. God cannot have a child since he does not have any desire for a wife. A third thing that has caused me to doubt the Bible is the writings and preaching of a Muslim scholar, Ahmad Deedat, who believes that the Bible has many problems.

Concerning the revelation of Allah, He revealed His Word, the Quran, to Muhammad through the angel Gabriel. This is the way God has revealed His words to Muhammad and the prophets before him. They all have asked us to do good and avoid bad. Why then shouldn't we follow Muhammad who is the last of the prophets? More than a billion people are following Muhammad in the world.

Isn't this in itself a proof of the greatness of Muhammad and Islam? On the other hand, there are non-Muslim writers, like Michael Heart, who writes good things about Muhammad.

Evaluation and Reply

Comments on Ali's Words

Ali's tone of response is much softer than before. His comments "*I must confess that some of the issues you have raised have taken me deep into thinking.*" and "*it is wonderful to be saved here.*" are indications of the positive impact of our conversations with him. I also sense his deeper heart cry suggesting that after all these years he has followed Islamic instructions for nothing: "Aren't they good enough to save people?"

There are also a few other things that are confusing Ali; he is fascinated by the great number of Muslims in the world. He has not thought that God is not impressed by numbers as much as quality. Another cause of his confusion is the observations of confused Muslim and non Muslim writers who have praised Islam without understanding the nature of Allah, the author of Islam.

Since I have sensed his deeper cry, I will respond to all the things he has mentioned, but my overriding focus will be on his question, "*What do you mean by sin?*"

Reply to Ali

It is encouraging that you have started to enjoy our conversation. This is the nature of open and creative dialogue. I pray that all peoples will understand the significance of openness and begin to read the chapters of each other's lives for better understanding and communication.

The nature of sin in Islam and in Christianity is more or less similar. The major difference is that in Islam sin has began before creation. It came into the world by Allah, but in Christianity sin began with human history and came into the world by Adam and Eve.

The belief about purity from sin is also another difference between these two religions. Purity in Islam means submitting to the daily prayers and religious rituals, but in Christianity it means having an eternal victory over sin. In Islam, you are pure but you still are not sure whether or not you will enter paradise, but in Christianity you are pure because you are saved, on your way to heaven and do not need to be concerned with Hell anymore, because the threat of Hell and Satan is cancelled by Jesus Christ. The Gospel says that Christ came to destroy the work of Satan in our lives (1 John 3: 8) and establish peace between God and us (Colossians 1:20). Every follower of Jesus Christ is delivered from Satan, redeemed to God (saved) and is in the safety of God's arms forever. So:

When you follow Muhammad, still you are not sure whether or not your sins are forgiven and whether or not you will go to heaven.

But when you trust in Christ, you are transformed from the kingdom of sin and Satan into the Kingdom of God. Your mind, heart and soul are destined for heaven and you live with Christ in the heavenly realm. Christ is in heaven. If you accept Jesus as your Lord and follow Him, you will be in heaven too. Your spiritual destiny is shaped by the one who leads you. If you follow a sinner (Muhammad), your status is sinfulness, but if you follow the sinless One (Jesus), your status is reckoned to be without sin.

So, faith in Christ not only guarantees the forgiveness of sin, but the impartation of a heavenly life as well. Not only we are forgiven, but we are also delivered from hell forever.

You asked my thoughts about the daily Islamic instructions, prayers, and rituals: Aren't they good enough to save?

You may be able to find some good things in religious rituals or in daily prayers, but they will not save you. There are two spiritual powers in this world that are opposed to each other: God and Satan. You are either in the Kingdom of God or in the kingdom of Satan. You cannot be in both in the same time. If you are in the Kingdom of God, you are saved and have one-hundred per cent confidence about your future. If you are not, you are in the kingdom of Satan. If so, who or what then can save you from the hands of Satan other than God? Nothing, and no one. For this reason, your prayer must only be to God, asking Him to save you from Satan. The difference between the prayers of Muslims and Christians can be summarized as follows:

The followers of Christ are saved, and they praise and worship God for their salvation. They also pray to God for the salvation of others. So, salvation is a reality in their life on earth.

Muslims pray so that they may be saved in the afterlife. In Islam salvation is not a part of this life so Muslims remain strangers to the Kingdom of God in this world. If God's Kingdom is absent in your heart, then the kingdom of Satan rules over it.

Muslims lack salvation even though they pray daily and follow daily rituals, but Christians are saved and do not need religious rituals anymore.

Even the Quran affirms that the Christians' future is assured and fear shall not come upon them (Q.2:62) and that they are above those who do not believe in Jesus, until the day of resurrection (Q.3:55). The Quran never states such a certainty about the future of Muhammad and his followers.

So, a sinner cannot submit himself to the holy God, unless his sins are forgiven, he is saved and his identity is a heavenly identity. In the same way, a Muslim also cannot submit himself to the sinless God unless he is made sinless first.

It is also wrong when you say that by coming to Islam your past sins will be wiped away. Imagine what would happen if a pagan killed a Christian or a Muslim and then became a Muslim. Are you saying that Islam would forgive him for that crime? If the answer is yes, then Islam encourages murder. If not, then his past sins are not forgiven.

Also, it is absolutely untrue to say that the sins of those who follow the sinless Christ will not be forgiven, but the sins of the followers of the sinful Muhammad will be forgiven. God is pleased if you follow a sinless One as your role model. In addition, submission to the sinless One is the proof of your honesty. The chance for the salvation of an honest people is greater than those who follow a sinner and are dishonest.

Please compare the following Christian beliefs with the Islamic ones you mentioned and see which one is superior. Christians believe:

In One God

In angels

In the personal revelation of God in addition to His words: God shows Himself to prophets, Jews and Christians.

In the words of the prophets of God

In the Judgment Day: those who are not saved here will be judged in front of the Throne of God and will go to Hell.

Salvation begins in this life on earth and continues for eternity

In eternal victory over Hell in this earthly life.

In the coming of Jesus Christ for judging the world and those who do not follow Him.

That evil does not come from God. Whatever comes from God is good and pure.

You also spoke about the five Islamic pillars and asked "*Aren't these good enough to protect Muslims from sin or to purify them?*" The following are responses to each Islamic pillar:

Witnessing

How can you be a witness for God if you are not saved by God and do not know Him? Salvation means that God has revealed Himself to you, and is sitting on the throne of your heart. If you do not have such a personal relationship with God and you do not know Him, then you are not a witness for Him. Moses and other prophets and apostles in the Bible saw God, spoke to Him face to face and knew Him. They were able to speak about God because of their personal relationship with God, yet Muhammad never saw God and therefore he and his followers cannot witness about God.

Prayer

God wants you to be saved first and then pray (or talk) to Him. For example, if your child has run away from you, your heart will not pleased until your child is back home; you hear and see him face to face when he is at home. In the same manner, your prayer is heard by God when you return to Him and ask Him to transform and purify you so that you can talk (pray) with Him. God cannot grant your request for forgiveness if you stay in the kingdom of impurity. So, to be at home (God's Kingdom) with God is the most important thing to God. For this reason, your first plea to God must be, "*Oh God, I want to make the Pure, Sinless and Perfect Jesus as my model; please transform me to be His follower and live like Him in your presence.*" After you accept Jesus as the leader of your life, God will grant your prayers because you have shown your seriousness in following the example of Jesus Christ's holiness, righteousness and love. This is what I did and God saved me, and I am with Him now and therefore have opportunity to talk and pray to Him.

So, your daily prayer to God must aim at being with God as soon as possible or it must originate from the state of your presence with God. Therefore, it is not because of a religious principle or pillar you have to pray to God but because of your urgent need for salvation or for thanksgiving or any other expression as the result of salvation.

Prayer is also something you can do every moment you are awake. It is a prayer of twenty-four hours a day, not only five times a day. Muslims pray to Allah only five times a day. Can you imagine how difficult the relationship would be with your family if you said to them, "*You are allowed to talk to me only five times a day and in my set times, but not at anytime you want.*

And you are only allowed to talk to me in Arabic even though you do not know the meaning of the words you use." Limiting prayer to God for only five times a day speaks of a limited relationship with God. Islamic prayer does not accommodate reality: God is closer than any one else to you and you do not need a memorized creed to talk to God or to express repentance to Him.

Another problem with Islamic prayer is that Muslims are not allowed to pray to Allah in their own mother tongue. Isn't Allah able to understand languages other than Arabic? Why should Muslims have to speak to Allah in Arabic only? Why does Allah disregard other languages? If it is easy for Allah to understand other languages, why does he make prayer more difficult for non-Arabic speaking Muslims? If prayer is from the heart, people will be able to pray better in their own mother tongues. In Christ, you can talk to God in your own mother tongue, because God knows and understands every language.

Charity

Charity is a good thing; it exists in Christianity as well as in Islam. In fact, "Christian" nations lead all others in giving to the poor and needy of the world. Christians believe that whatever they have belongs to God and should be shared with the less fortunate. Because of this Judeo-Christian value, many western countries extend a helping hand even to poor Muslim nations. However, Charity in Islam is given only to needy Muslims; it is not given to non-Muslims. Jesus has taught us to help all humankind who are in need no matter what their beliefs, nationalities and races are. God has created the world as a community and expects the members of this community to help each other. Clearly, charity does not save anyone's soul. You cannot save your soul by giving money or food to the poor. It is not charity for your prodigal child that opens your door to him, but your unconditional love for him. You take him into your house because you want him at home with you. It is the same with God. He wants you to be with Him. One He can save you. Your charity cannot save you though you gave all your wealth to others. Indeed, all pagans in the world help each other. Do you think that their charity will save them at the Resurrection? Nothing can save people but the unconditional love of God. Jesus said, "*Seek first the kingdom of God*" (Matthew 6:33). You need to be saved first and then give gladly to others.

Fasting

Fasting is also good. However, abstaining from food cannot purify your soul. Your soul can only be purified when you acknowledge Jesus—the spotless One—as the Lord of your heart. If you follow Muhammad or Moses or Abraham as a role model, you will sin again because they were all sinners. But when the Spirit of Jesus Christ fills your heart, the desire for sin or to follow Satan is driven out. Hence, the presence of Jesus Christ releases you and purifies your heart.

Let me ask you a question about fasting. If fasting purifies, why wasn't then Muhammad sure about his future, since purification means righteousness and righteous ones go to paradise? Muhammad himself knew that his fasting was not going to save his soul, and for this reason he said "Allah-o-Aalam", only Allah knows.

Christians do not fast in order to please God so that He will save them. They fast because they are saved. Fasting, therefore, is an indication of salvation and is an expression of appreciation to God for what He has done for us in saving us. We can also fast to be a blessing to others. For example, we might not eat in order to give our food or the equivalent in money to the needy. We might fast for the salvation or healing of others or even for peace with our enemies. We might fast to better understand the suffering of those who live in hunger.

Pilgrimage

Like all other pillars of Islam, pilgrimage also does not save you. God is not only in Mecca. He is everywhere. He is just now standing beside you where you are, and is knocking on the door of your heart, waiting for you to open your heart and invite

Him in. When He comes into your heart, then Satan leaves you. Wherever God resides, there is no place for Satan. This is called purification and salvation, which is the faith of Christ. For this reason, you need Jesus in your heart—He cleanses us from all sin and purifies our heart.

In your response, you also said, "*Muslims wash themselves before prayers, but you Christians do not do that. How then you can pray to the holy God since you are not clean?*"

You need to know that sin is spiritual; it cannot be washed with water. Sin can only be cleansed by Christ, the One who is pure from all sin. So, by washing yourself on the outside you will not be able to cleanse yourself spiritually, on the inside. Your stomach is full of those things that are called unclean by Islam. Let me turn your question back to you and ask, "*How can you pray to the holy God since your intestine is full of unclean things?*"

A Godly purification is a spiritual purification, which takes place in the heart. For this reason, we need to ask the Lord, with his complete holiness, into our hearts. This is the only way that we can be united with a holy God in order to have fellowship with Him, worship and praise Him. Another benefit of spiritual purification is that you can always be in contact with God. The followers of Christ are purified through Christ, are with God and can speak (or pray) to Him always.

You asked my view about any chance of salvation for a Muslim who sincerely repents to Allah. Let me express my view by asking you some questions. Is there any Muslim in the world who is closer to Allah than Muhammad? An Islamic response is, "Obviously not". Didn't Muhammad sincerely repent to Allah? Your answer is, "Yes". Why then was he not sure that his sins would be forgiven and that he would enter paradise? Please see what Muhammad has said concerning his afterlife:

> *Muhammad said: "The good deeds of any person will not make him enter Paradise." The Prophet's companions said, "Not even you, O Allah's Apostle?" He said, "Not even myself, unless Allah*

> *bestows His favor and mercy (rahma) on me."* (Bukhari 7: 70; 577; also read Q.46:9)
>
> *Narrated Masruq: I said to 'Aisha, "O Mother! Did Prophet Muhammad see his Lord?" Aisha said, "What you have said makes my hair stand on end ! Know that if somebody tells you one of the following three things, he is a liar: Whoever tells you that Muhammad saw his Lord, is a liar." Then Aisha recited the Verse: 'No vision can grasp Him, but His grasp is over all vision. He is the Most Courteous Well-Acquainted with all things.' (6.103) 'It is not fitting for a human being that Allah should speak to him except by inspiration or from behind a veil.' (42.51) 'Aisha further said, "And whoever tells you that the Prophet knows what is going to happen tomorrow, is a liar." She then recited: 'No soul can know what it will earn tomorrow'* (31.34) … (Bukhari 6 :60 :378)

No Muslim, including Muhammad and all others who sincerely repent, is sure that his sin will be forgiven by Allah. As I have mentioned earlier, the problem in Islam is at the root of Islam. Since Allah created sin, Muslims will not be able to avoid sin no matter how repentant they may be. And this will always prevent them from having assurance about their future. The only solution is that they need to forsake Allah, the god of the Quran, and follow the God of the Bible who is holy, just, loving and a Savior.

By the way, why do Muslims need to repent to Allah and ask his forgiveness for sins when Allah himself is the cause of their sin? Logically, it is Allah who is the creator of sin and needs to repent! Indeed, Allah cannot be called merciful or generous because he has created the sins and disasters of the world. The best mercy is when you keep the world away from sin, and Allah was not able to do that.

You also said, "*Allah has promised us a beautiful future … why shouldn't we believe that his ways are the perfect way?*"

Logically, the teaching of Islam cannot be perfect if its author, Allah, is the creator of sin and disaster, which are against perfection. The teaching of the Bible is perfect, because whatever the God of the Bible created from the beginning was good and without sin. Sin and disaster appeared in the world after Adam and Eve sinned. God, who hates sin, took initiative through Jesus Christ in order to save the world form sin.

Concerning the revelation of God's words in the Bible, God Himself revealed His words to the prophets of the Bible directly for most of the time. The personal revelation of God is logical too. If God's presence is everywhere, He can have personal relationships with people and speak to any one. The Bible says that God even spoke to the Israelites (Deuteronomy 4:12, 33, 36). Why? Because He prefers a direct relationship and desires to speak directly and personally. Those who had a direct and personal relationship with God can witness for God, but not Muhammad who did not see God. Even your Quran says that Jesus is in heaven and with God. The Quran does not say such a thing about Muhammad. Hence, Jesus can speak with authority about God and heaven more than any other prophet.

The reason that Muhammad cannot be in line with the prophets of the Bible is because he followed Allah who is the creator of sin, whereas the prophets of the Bible followed the God who is holy and just and cannot create sin. Also, the prophets of the Bible were sure about their eternal destiny; Muhammad was not.

You also said that more than a billion people in the world are following Muhammad and this in itself is a proof of Muhammad's greatness. Your numeric logic can work against you. What if we said that, "*There are billions of non-Muslims who do not follow Muhammad, which proves the greatness of non-Islamic belief.*" In addition, all evidence in Islam shows that there will be more people in hell than Muslims in heaven. According to your mathematical calculation, does this argue that Satan is greater than Muhammad? My friend, God is not impressed with numbers. He is impressed when you give your heart to Him and when a lost person turns his (her) face to Him and asks Him for salvation.

I see that you are wondering if Muhammad was not a genuine prophet, how could Michael Heart write about him positively or Ahmad Deedat invest his life in his path. Well, all other religions have similar situations. Religious scholars are not our final authority; we have an obligation to examine the truthfulness of our beliefs. I don't think that Heart and Deedat were challenged with the questions I have raised in our dialogue so far. Deedat's writings are all about superficial things. Deedat does not discuss the fundamental differences between the Qur'an and the Bible, or Allah and the God of the Bible—things we have discussed so far. He did not know enough to discuss the root of Islam and Christianity, and for this reason he only brushed the branches of these religions and throughout his entire life confused many people.

God is the God of all. He has created you in such a way that you can use your own mind, heart and conscience to read and discover Him personally. You do not need a Deedat or Heart since you were created to discover the truth for yourself. This is what we've done so far: we have asked fundamental questions, discussed them and considered possible answers to them. I could wish that Deedat could also have been confronted with these questions and have discovered the amazing characteristics of the one true God. If he had, he would not have spent his time with superficial and untrue things at all.

In response to your belief about Jesus as a man and unable to save others I want to say to you that salvation is only for those who are sinners. Even your Quran cannot attribute any sin to Jesus and also comments that He is perfect and in heaven. Any one who is already in heaven does not need salvation.

Why is Jesus sinless? Because when the Holy Spirit overshadowed Mary, by a supernatural miracle, she became pregnant with the perfect, sinless, Holy Spirit. Jesus was not the seed of a sinful man, as Muhammad was.

How is Jesus able to save sinful men and take them to heaven?

Because He was from heaven and ascended into heaven, He has the authority to lead you and I into heaven. As I have mentioned to you earlier: By contrast, Satan belongs to hell and has dragged mankind with him through the fall; Jesus belongs to heaven and has invited mankind to heaven with Him through His death for their sin and through his resurrection for their justification. In other words, Jesus came to rescue sinners from their sin and Satan's captivity. As you mentioned, "*it is wonderful to be saved here*", Jesus came to this world to do this wonderful thing for all.

According to the Quran, if you follow Muhammad, you will be taken to hell first and then maybe to heaven (Q.19:68-72). However, if you follow Jesus, who is in heaven, you are headed to heaven for sure, forever. You will never be taken to hell after death, but you will be taken directly to heaven. The Path of Christ is so different from the path of Muhammad.

Jesus is not a mere man. Jesus is the Spirit of God who became Man. The Bible calls Him the spiritual "Son of God," because He is the Son of the Spirit and is the "Word of God." The Gospel says:

> *Flesh gives birth to flesh, but the Spirit gives birth to spirit* (John 3:6).

For this reason, His Spirit is the divine Spirit of God who became Man and dwelt among us for the sake of our salvation and for the destruction of the work of Satan. If Muslim scholars and evangelists would carefully consider and analyze the theological implications of relevant Quranic verses, they could not deny the divinity of Jesus Christ. Even the Quran teaches the birth of Jesus Christ as the result of the coming of the Word and Spirit of God upon the Virgin Mary, not as the result of a sexual relationship (Q.3:45,47; 4.171; 19:17; 21:91). Oddly, Muhammad learned the contents of these verses from the church. As the Islamic traditions show us, he went to church for many years with and without his first wife, Khadijah. That's why these verses of the Qur'an appear to be more closely related to biblical beliefs regarding Jesus' conception than to many fanciful Islamic notions that have been floating around in the thoughts of Muslim evangelists throughout Islam's history. So, Jesus is sinless, divine, in heaven and the Savior of all mankind. For this reason, God wanted Mary to call Him Jesus, which means "Savior," and "Emanuel," which means "God with us. "

Some Muslim scholars believe that "the Spirit of God (Holy Spirit) sent to the Virgin Mary" in Q.19:17 is the arch-angel Gabriel who became Jesus. The Quran does not confirm this; it explicitly denies it.

> *Before you* (Muhammad) *We* (Allah) *have only send men as messengers whom We have inspired* (Q.16:43).

Allah is saying to Muhammad that his messengers or prophets or apostles, including Muhammad, were all from mankind—the seed of man, not an angel. Jesus is neither the seed of man nor the seed of an angel; He is "the Word" and "the Spirit of God," which means God Himself.

According to the Bible, as in the Qur'an, it is blasphemous to believe in more than One God. There is no other god but Yahweh—the God of the Bible. Contrary to what Muslims think, the Trinity is not three gods, but the revelation of One God in three Persons. God is a personal God and He reveals Himself with personalities in different roles just as we humans have personalities and reveal ourselves with the roles of fathers, husbands, wives, sons and daughters. Christians, therefore, do not believe in three gods. This is propaganda from the later revelations of Muhammad and from Muslim scholars who have attempted to misrepresent the truth of the Bible in order to justify their erroneous doctrines.

Ali's Fifth Response

I was trying to bring you back to Islam, but you have established yourself in wisdom and logic powerfully and are able to prove your stand in truth strongly. Hold to your faith strongly and also remember me in your prayers. You are an eye-opener.

The Result

Ali was a leader in a mosque. He had 300 pupils, teaching them the Quran and helping them to memorize it. He gradually withdrew from this activity and later gave his heart to the Lord. His extended family members and friends discovered his faith and plotted to kill him. He had no choice but to escape from his hometown to a big city far from his Muslim friends and family. He said to me that he had lost everything, but is joyful in the Lord.

Conclusion

PART V

18

No Salvation without the Trinity

The Trinity (God the Father, the Son and the Holy Spirit) describes God's full revelation and His full purpose in remedying the devastating effects of sin in men's lives, in their relationships with each other and with God. The Trinity is absolutely necessary to save people from the bondage of their sin and provides a reasonable, just, perfect, and everlasting freedom from that bondage.

Each person of the Trinity has a mission that reveals the eternal and unconditional love of God for people to have peace and freedom. The Trinity proves that God is personal, omnipresent, and accessible so that people can call upon Him to save them.

Paul, the Apostle of Jesus Christ, writes that the ministry of the Holy Spirit is to breathe into men and women's hearts a knowledge of God through a living relationship with Jesus Christ. (1 Corinthians 2:10-16). He calls these men and women "*an epistle of Christ, ministered by us, written not with ink but by **the Spirit of the living God**, not on tablets of stone but on tablets of flesh, that is, of the heart*" (2 Corinthians 3:3); a letter of freedom from Christ for the world, or "*the fragrance of His knowledge in every place*" (2 Corinthians 2:14). Paul writes that Christ has paid the price for freedom, redeeming Christians from the lord of evil—Satan—and removing the blindness ("veils") that once covered their minds and hearts so that they can have knowledge of God, be reconciled with Him, receive His righteousness and freedom, and also minister to others to need that freedom too (2 Corinthians 5:17-21). He writes:

> *Whenever it* (the heart of a person) *turns to* ***the Lord*** **(Jesus)**, *the veil shall be taken away. And* ***the Lord is that Spirit****; and where the Spirit of the Lord is, there is liberty*" (2 Corinthians 3:16-17). "*...by which* (the Spirit) *we cry, Abba, Father. The Spirit Himself bears witness with our spirit that we are the children of God*" (Romans 8:15-16; Galatians 4:6).

In his letter to the Corinthians, Paul calls those people, who distinguish the difference between God and idols and are not yoked together with idol worshipers, His sons and daughters (2 Corinthians 6:14-18).

Notice that the verses above—only a few of the many verses in the Bible—address *God, Jesus and the Spirit as one and the same.* There is no difference in their essence, only in their mission. In essence, God is one and unique. He is called Father, Son, or the Holy Spirit only because of His various missions towards mankind:

> *There is ...one Spirit...one Lord... one God and Father of all* (Ephesians 4:4-6).

The mission of the Trinity is to relate to every aspect of men's and women's lives and challenge their minds, hearts and consciences so they may get rid of any lawlessness or unrighteousness in their lives. Trinity establishes a 'spiritual court' in people's hearts, reveals Himself as the full example of righteousness, holiness and justice, challenging them to get rid of Satan, the source of lawlessness. So the Trinity makes salvation accessible in life on earth, contrary to the world religions that introduce salvation as an impractical theory inaccessible in this life. Jesus said;

> *Now is the judgment of this world. Now shall the prince of this world be cast out … I have come as a Light into the world, so that whoever believes on Me should not remain in darkness* (John 12:31, 46).

Those religions that relegate the salvation of people until the afterlife are, consciously or unconsciously, rejecting the fulfillment of God's justice on earth and in this way supporting the spread of immorality. People, to avoid immorality and unrighteousness, need the full revelation of God's absolute justice and truth in all dimensions of his life on earth. This unchains him from the dominion of Satan, purifies his thoughts, words and deeds and enables him to walk with God in righteousness.

So, the biblical revelation of a Triune God rids the lawless work of Satan in the lives of people and releases them, and brings them into an intimate relationship with God. This freedom from Satan's dominion takes place in the human heart where evil and temptation once reigned, now the righteousness and justice of God can reign. Through a ruling of the Triune God, the believing human heart has become a 'spiritual court' where God's justice is taken to victory and His holiness and love take precedence.

Who is qualified to sit on the throne of justice in this spiritual court in the human heart and take justice to victory; God, humanity itself or Satan? Is any man or woman qualified to be the judge in this court? Has any person in the world (including prophets) ever obeyed God to absolute perfection and are absolutely moral, wise enough and capable enough to defend the case for God, whose right is breached by humankind and Satan? No! As the book of Job says;

> *Will you* (as betrayer) *lift up His person, or content for God?* (Job 13:8b)
>
> *Shall one who hates right govern? And will you condemn Him who is just and mighty?* (Job 34:17b)

Sin or immorality or unrighteousness is a problem in every person's life. People are in bondage to unrighteousness and cannot stand before God who is absolutely moral and righteous. Secondly, people are guilty of cooperating with Satan. Thirdly, people need a more powerful force to unchain them from Satan, the lawless one. Last but certainly not least, imperfect humanity is not able to defend God's perfect law of justice. For these reasons, it is above and beyond the capacity of people to undertake the task of judgment against Satan to save themselves.

As a result, Religions that require their people to be righteous or to act righteously before salvation are irrational and unrealistic since they are not cleared from their lawless cases against God.

Satan also cannot be the judge in this spiritual court, since he is the source of lawlessness. **It is only God who is able to establish the court and be the judge over it.**

Why would God, whose laws were breached by humankind, be interested in establishing such justice in this world in order to rescue people? The only reason that the Bible gives is the love of God towards humankind. He has created humankind for Himself and loves them. **God's love—along with His justice—is another motivation behind His will to rescue people and remove the lawlessness from their hearts.**

One reason that God is called 'Father' in the Bible is because through His Fatherly love He births new life in spiritual dead people and makes them brothers and sisters—members of one body, one family and one kingdom. So the Spirit of Fatherhood takes the responsibility to rescue people from the bondage of Satan, the prince of lawlessness, and restore them into His Kingdom.

Can people be released without paying the cost for his sins and lawlessness? A just religion cannot release a sinful person without covering the cost of his sin. Because humanity had free will, and with this free will chose to break God's law, it now has to pay the cost. Justice cannot ignore the cost of lawlessness.

Again the question rises here; can a person cover the cost of his sins and save himself? The response is 'no'. He is spiritually dead. A dead person cannot bring himself back to life. Is there any one else who can pay the cost for a spiritually dead person and rescue him? Using the same logic as above, God is the only source that can pay the cost for a human being and release him.

God's Fatherly love motivates Him to pay the price for humanity's salvation. Since people are spiritually dead and cannot reach out to God, the only solution is for God to reach out to humanity. God entered this lawless world (the world of death), paid the price on the Cross, breaking down the barrier (Satan) between humankind and Himself, making the spiritual resurrection from death to life possible. He revealed Himself as the Son and redeemed humanity, announcing victory over death. In other words, one of the three persons of God, the Son Jesus, was incarnated for the purpose of giving His life as a ransom for sinners so that they may be released from the bondage of Satan and approach God with freedom and confidence.

In the beginning, people were with God; however, Satan deceived them to abuse their freedom, drew them out of the kingdom of God and placed them into the kingdom of death. But this time, God as Son entered the kingdom of death and brought people back into His kingdom, to be with Him. Though Satan killed people spiritually, Jesus brought them back to life spiritually. While Satan made people lawless, Jesus brought them back into lawfulness. While Satan stripped the loving attitudes from the human heart and mind and filled people with hatred, hostility and bloodshed, Jesus took them back to His kingdom and clothed them with love.

The Holy Spirit is the third person that is revealed in the Trinity. God is holy and his holiness is a tool He uses to implant His love and justice into the human heart. In other words, God not only calls people to be holy, but also regenerates them in His holiness enabling them to live a totally new life. People cannot be holy unless they are transferred from the dominion of sin into the dominion of righteousness. Contrary to the teachings of other religions, sin, in Christianity is not a wrong act but a wrong being that leads to wrong doing. Therefore, it is first of all, men's identity, not their actions that needs to be changed. If they are not rescued from the dominion of Satan, they will not be able to do good. However, when the holiness of God is implanted into their hearts, they are convicted of their ungodliness, and led to accept God's justice and the ransom He paid for their release. This is the sovereign work and choice of God through His triune personalities. In other words, the Trinity first changes the identity into righteousness and then calls them to act righteous. If the Holy God (The Holy Spirit) is not in the human heart, people will not be able to act righteously.

Not only did God love people and pay the penalty for their transgressions, releasing them from the bondage of Satan, but He also resides in the life of people as the Holy Guardian, Teacher, Leader, Protector, Speaker and Sanctifier in order to fill them with love, joy, peace, patience, kindness, goodness, faithfulness, gentleness and self-control (Galatians 5:22). As Paul, the disciple of Christ, said;

> *For God has not called us to uncleanness, but in sanctification. Therefore he who despises does not despise man, but* ***God, who also has given us His Holy Spirit*** (1 Thessalonians 4:7-8).
>
> *God has from the beginning chosen you to salvation through sanctification of the* ***Spirit*** *and belief of the truth, to which He called you by our gospel, to the obtaining of the glory of our Lord Jesus Christ … Now may our* ***Lord Jesus Christ*** *Himself, and* ***God, even our Father****, who has loved us and has given us everlasting consolation and good hope through grace, comfort your hearts and establish you in every good word and work* (2 Thessalonians 2:13b-14, 16-17).

Therefore, the God of universe revealed His intimate triune personalities in three persons in order to release people, give them new life and empower them with His qualities. In biblical terminology, God is called Father, Son and the Holy Spirit but all are One and eternal (Deuteronomy 32:6; 33:27; Psalms

2:7; John 1:1; 10:30; Romans 9:5b; 2 Corinthians 3:14-18; Ephesians 4:6; Titus 2:13; Hebrew 1:8; 9:14; 13:8; 2 Peter 1:1; Revelation 1:18):

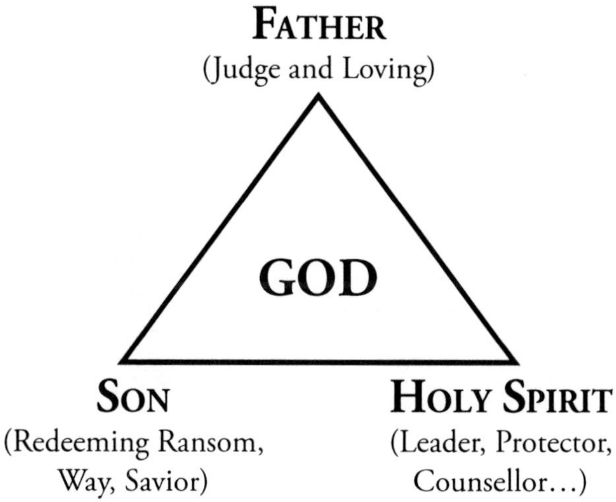

It is through the Revelation of God's triune persons, who are one in essence, that people can be released and empowered in all dimensions of life:

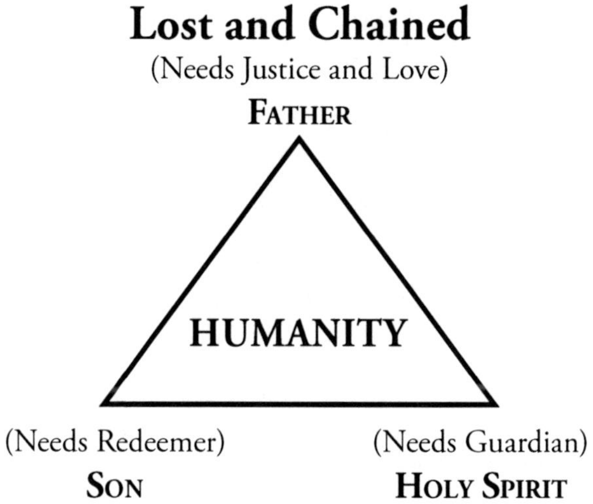

Humanity is lost and chained and in need of a redeemer and guardian. A lost person needs a loving guardian, someone who intimately and tirelessly pays the cost to release him and give him further help and protection. Someone who loves, nurtures, guides, encourages, teaches and does everything within his power to equip his child for life. If a parent would use all his abilities, attributes and wealth to find his lost and troubled child, how much more would God, in all His being, labor for the one whom He loves and has created for Himself?

Who can be the good, caring guardian other than the mighty God, who is the source of unconditional love? Who can, other than God, give eternal assurance and confidence to a lost humanity?

When can lost humanity take shelter in God and call Him Father? The answer is, "Only when God **reveals** Himself fully and personally".

The full revelation of God to save human beings is only comprehensible through the Trinity. The following words of Christ clearly illustrate the above:

> *And the slave does not abide in the house forever, but the Son abides forever* (John 8:35).
>
> ***I*** *will not leave you orphans. I will come to you …* ***We*** *will come to him and make Our abode with him … the Comforter, the* ***Holy Spirit*** *whom the Father will send in My name, He shall teach you all things and bring all things to your remembrance, whatever I have said to you. Peace I leave with you, My peace I give to you. Not as the world gives do I give to you. Let not your heart be troubled, neither let it be afraid* (John 14:18, 23, 26, 27).
>
> *And when the Comforter has come, whom I will send to you from the Father, the Spirit of truth who proceeds from the Father, He shall testify of Me* (John 15:26).

Jesus said to His followers that He would not leave them orphans or fatherless. His words bring forth the meaning that He will be coming daily to His followers in His Triune personalities (Father, Son and Holy Spirit), will visit them through His grace and in this way give them peace.

Without the Trinity, life is dangerous and hostile. Jesus made clear in His words the reason for the hostility of those Jews who aimed to kill Him. It was because they were not the children of God; they were Fatherless spiritually. If they had known God and belonged to Him, then they would have recognized Jesus for who He really was and given Him the honor He deserved—sent from God, the Son of God—God in the flesh! Jesus said to them:

> *You seek to kill Me ... If God* (*the judge*, v.50) *were your Father, you would love Me ... and you dishonor Me* (John 8:40, 42, 49).

So, the Message of Christ is to challenge and open the minds of people in order to understand that God is personal and that His Triune[1] personalities are of vital importance for transferring people from hostility into caring, loving and peaceful attitudes (fatherliness).

The revelation of Jesus Christ is not like the natural birth of humankind that born into the human race or made of dust as in the case of Adam. In His revelation, God comes from Above, becomes Man in His absolute perfection and enters into human history. He, therefore, is not from this world and cannot be equated (as in the case of Islam and other religions) with any who are of this world, since we are all made of dust and once

---

1 Just as a parent can be called loving towards his child, a redeemer and helper, so is God as Father (lover), Son (redeemer) and Holy Spirit (helper). Tri-unity can be discovered in many things and places. Water is ice, liquid and steam; time is future, present and past; man is father, son and husband; woman is mother, daughter and wife. Every person is soul, spirit and body (1 Thessalonians 3:23). Each personality manifests itself for the particular position and role, but they are all one in essence and united in one person or thing.

dead, return again to dust. Unlike the man of this world, Jesus is from and in heaven, and in control of everything.

Problems, Questions & Answers

Why is God called "The Son" in His redeeming mission? Couldn't He simply be called God in all His missions for mankind?

The Bible uses the word "Son" to describe God as a **personal** God who can **reveal** Himself in all dimensions of human life in order to make Himself knowable to reconcilable to them:

> … (Jesus) *is the image of the invisible God, the First-born of all creation. For all things were created in Him, the things in the heavens, and the things on the earth, the visible and the invisible, whether thrones or dominions or principalities or powers, all things were created through Him and for Him. And He is before all things, and by Him all things consist. And He is the Head of the body, the church, who is the Beginning, the First-born from the dead, that He may be pre-eminent in all things.* ***For it pleased the Father that in Him*** (Jesus) ***all fullness should dwell****. And through Him having made peace through the blood of His cross, it pleased the Father to reconcile all things to Himself through Him, whether the things on earth or the things in Heaven* (Colossians 1:15-20).

In Jesus, God revealed Himself personally in order to have personal relationship with humankind, reconciling them to Himself and to one another as the absolute source of peace. God is personal and is able to reach humankind since humankind is in the bondage of Satan and unable to reach God.

Jesus Himself has also given many proofs about His equality with God (the Father), by doing the works that only God do (Matthew 5:43-48; John 5:21-30; 6:40; 11:38-39, 43-44; Acts 1:3). He said:

> "*I and the Father are one.*" "*I am the Son of God*". "*Father is in Me, and I in Him*". "*For whatever things He does, these*

> *also the Son does likewise." "He gives eternal life"* (John 10:30, 36c-38; 5:19; 17:2).

His disciples, who lived with Him and saw Him after the resurrection, all approved His equality with God. Peter said;

> *For not having followed fables having been cunningly devised, but becoming eyewitnesses of the majesty of Jesus Christ, we made known to you the power and coming of our Lord. For He received honor and glory from God the Father, when was borne to Him a voice from the excellent glory, "This is My beloved Son, in whom I am well pleased." And we heard this voice being borne from Heaven, being with Him in the holy mountain* (2 Peter 1:16-18).

Paul, who once was one of the persecutors of the early church because of its belief in Jesus as God, saw the risen Jesus (1 Corinthians 15:8-9). This encounter completely convinced him that Jesus and Father were one and the same Creator of all things:

> *There is to us only one God, the Father, of whom are all things, and we in Him; and one Lord Jesus Christ, through whom are all things, and we by Him* (1 Corinthians 8:6; read Colossians 1:15-17).

19

A Call to Follow Christ

Conscience can Discern the Truth

Do you believe that God is Holy? If your answer is "yes", then this is "yes" to Christianity and "no" to all other religions, since it is only in Christianity that God is holy. In eastern religions, the devil is in god's own nature, and in Islam, it is Allah who has corrupted Satan and created sin in humankind. So, these gods cannot be holy.

Do you believe that God must be the source of all certainty? If your response is "yes", then it is "yes" to Christianity and "no" to all other religions, because the dualistic nature of gods in other religions has made them unable to provide assurance to their followers. If you ask a follower of Christ, "Are you saved?" The response will be, "Yes, of course", whereas in all other religions, no one is certain of his/her present and future spiritual position.

Do you have a holy relationship with the real God? Do you want to have fellowship with God and be with Him from now until eternity? Do you want to be identified with God and be His salt and light among the nations of the world standing for His perfect peace, love and justice? If your response is "yes", therefore, it is necessary for you to search first for the real God, understand Him and then commit yourself to Him and get into a living relationship with Him.

Do you believe that the random life in world philosophies will provide a bright future for you? If your response is "no," then follow Jesus.

Your conscience is the only part of your being which is capable of discerning the truth. Listen to your conscience, distinguish the truth from falsehood by reflecting on these concluding words and decide which path you ought to follow.

Gods Made in Humanity's Image

Gods who are the sources of sin and spiritual darkness are impure gods. An impure god cannot be a real God but a man-made image, a mixture of light and darkness. How can such a god be trusted? In fact, a god with this characteristic cannot exist.

In **Hinduism**, people are taught to cherish desires in their hearts and meditate on these gods in order to be absorbed in or join them. However, people are not aware that their own spiritual position is better than their gods. If we show a Hindu's spiritual being with this sign ◑ and Brahman with the larger circle below, we will be able to understand why a shift from the position of human to god is both dangerous and irrational. Humanity, as a little manifestation of a great god, has a fairly small amount of darkness compared to that god. In light of this comparison, why would someone wish to have a shift from a relatively bad position to an extremely worse one?

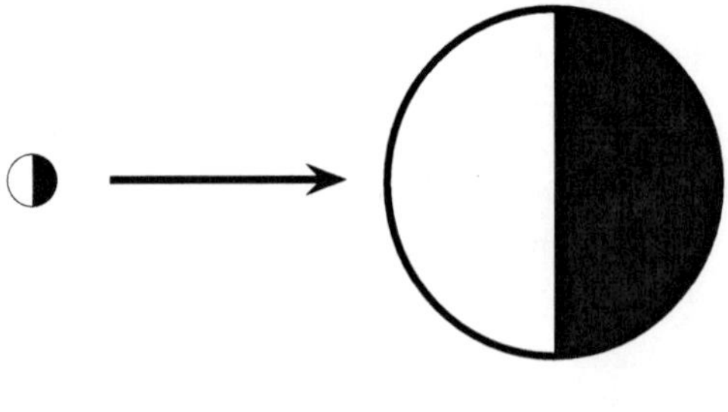

Hindu God
(The Source of Impurity)

In **Theravada Buddhism** god and everything else is the creation of the mind and is not real. If this is the case, Buddha's advice cannot be real as it is the product of his own mind. It contains much uncertainty and confusion.

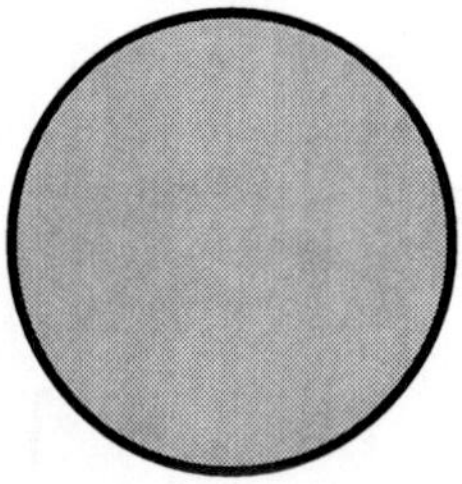

God in Buddhism
(Product of Mind)

In **Islam**, though Allah is called holy and pure, he is described as the creator of sin in Satan and in human beings. This dualistic doctrine does not present Allah as just and holy. How can the Holy God want people to be sinners? If Allah has created people sinners and unrighteous, he cannot require them to be righteous. However, as previously mentioned, purity cannot inspire impurity. It is impurity that begets impurity.

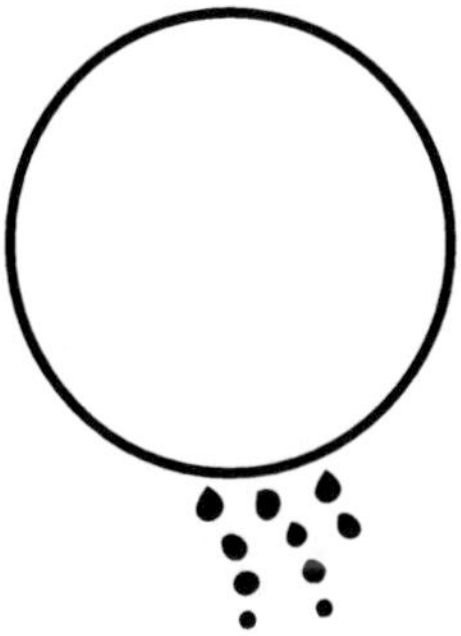

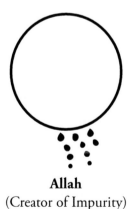

Allah
(Creator of Impurity)

In **Christianity**, God is holy and pure. From the beginning, His creation resembles His nature. He cannot create sin nor have partnership with sin, nor with sinners. Sin entered into people through Satan's temptation, separating them from God. People are in need of a Savior as they are unable to save themselves from the captivity of Satan. God, as the source of all purity, provides a clear path for people which leads to salvation.

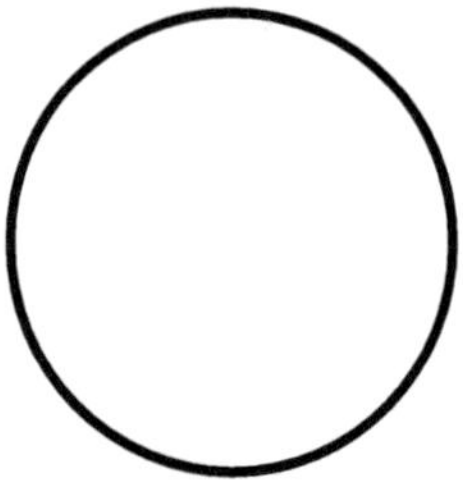

Pure God (Jesus)
(The Absolute Source of Purity)

The Heavens Compared

In Christianity, people have to be completely purified in order to enter heaven. If we illustrate a person as a rectangle and heaven as a circle, heaven in Christianity can be portrayed as follows;

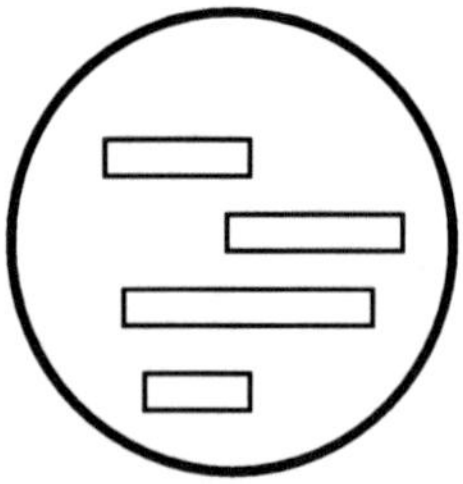

Heaven with Purity

In other religions heaven is not immune to sin. For example, Islam believes that if the righteousness of a person outweighs his unrighteousness he will then enter heaven. Therefore, it is unnecessary for the complete purification of humanity as illustrated below:

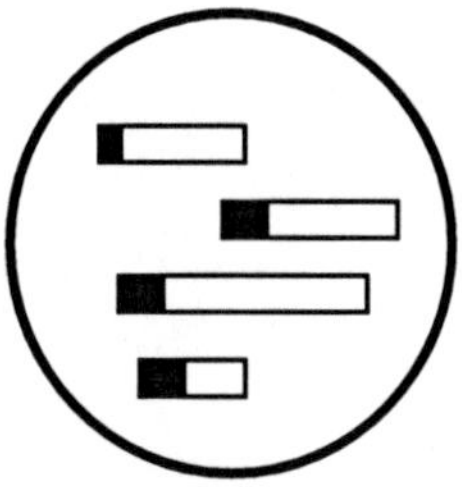

Heaven with Impurity

The above diagram shows that darkness (sin) has entered paradise (heaven) through humankind. There is no paradise with black spots of sin in it. Such a paradise does not equate with the holiness of God. We know that darkness can in no way exist in a pure heaven. A heaven with impurity cannot be real. Heaven, by definition, is the place of absolute purity and perfection. It is the dwelling place of the Holy God. It is a place for those who have allowed the Holy God to completely drive Satan out from their lives and release them from his dominion.

Why then does Allah allow Muslims, who are not purified and do not believe in complete purification, to enter paradise (heaven) and have partnership with him? If Allah is pure, how can he have partnership with the unpurified?

The answer is obvious. Allah is not pure—he has partnership with sin.

How is Good and Bad Weighed?

How can it be that other religions compare good and bad in order to determine which outweighs the other? What good acts can outweigh bad acts such as murder or rape? Can giving your wealth to charity remove the effect of your crime on victims or their families?

By breaking a human heart, you have also broken God's heart, as He created humankind for Himself and loves them with His whole being. You cannot win God's heart with your so-called good deeds unless you allow God to renew you so that you are no longer a threat to society. It is only through God that this transformation is possible. This, in turn, delivers you from all self-centeredness, destroying the transgressions of your mind and heart, releasing you from their bondages. This supernatural transformation results in the absolute justice, love, and purity of God to you and renews you completely in all dimensions of your life. It places the love of God into your heart, creating a faith that says without the absolute love of God you are nothing, thus expelling the whole notion of weighing good and bad. As Paul, the disciple of Christ, says, *"When perfection comes, the imperfect disappears".* Or to put it in other words, "When good (Christ) comes, bad (Satan) disappears":

> *Though I speak with the tongues of men and of angels, and have not charity, I have become as sounding brass or a tinkling cymbal. And though I have prophecies, and understand all mysteries and all knowledge; and though I have all faith, so as to move mountains, and do not have charity, I am nothing. And though I give out all my goods to feed the poor, and though I deliver my body to be burned, and have not charity, I am profited nothing. Charity has patience, is kind; charity is not envious, is not vain, is not puffed up; does not behave indecently, does not seek her own, is not easily provoked, thinks no evil. Charity does not rejoice in unrighteousness, but rejoices in the truth, quietly covers all things, believes all things, hopes all things, endures all things. Charity never fails. But if there are prophecies, they will be abolished; if tongues, they shall cease; if knowledge, it will be abolished. For we know in part, and we prophesy in part. But when the perfect thing comes, then that which is in part will be caused to cease* (1 Corinthians 13:1-10).

The theories of salvation in all other religions are impractical according to the Gospel of Jesus Christ since they hold the notion that unpurified and imperfect humanity can enter a perfect heaven, or paradise. The heaven of a holy God cannot be receptive toward men and women who are still slave to sin in the life on earth. In no way can a trace of darkness be found in a holy God's heaven. In Christ, a person must be completely purified and cut off from his relationship with Satan prior to entering heaven. This proves that salvation and freedom in Christ is a perfect salvation.

The Salt and Light of the World

A purified person, the person whose relationship with Satan is completely annulled, can play a significant role and become a good spiritual, moral and ethical example of truthful living before others. A person with such characteristics is only found among the followers of Christ.

The Gospel of Jesus Christ claims that peace and love come from a pure heart, a good conscience, and a sincere faith, which encourage understanding and affirm confidence (1 Timothy 1:3-7). It maintains that the church of Christ can make the manifold wisdom of God known to the nations of the world (Ephesians 3:7-10).

Why would the followers of Christ be chosen for such a great task? The followers of Christ, unlike the followers of all other religions, have a pure God and Savior, a pure heaven, a purified life and a certain and perfect salvation and thus they provide a good example for life among all the nations. In Christianity, life is centered on and led by purity, whereas in other religions impurity is the source of life. Gods in other religions are impure in their nature, so too are their paradises. They have instructed their followers to rely on their own impure human strength to achieve purity. But the fact remains that impurity cannot and does not lead to purity.

The Bible provides some unique characteristics of Christians that set them apart as the salt and light of the world:

1. The church (the followers of Christ) is purified of sin, unchained from the dominion of Satan and have approached God with freedom and confidence through faith in Jesus Christ

(Ephesians 3:11-12). So the followers of Christ have been clothed in real freedom and can proclaim it to others.

2. The wisdom that has been given to the church comes from God and it is pure, peace-loving, considerate, submissive, full of mercy and sincerity. Peacemakers who sow in peace raise a harvest of righteousness (James 3:17-18). So the followers of Christ have received their peace-loving wisdom from God, the source of absolute love. Through Christ, they have been reconciled to God, transferred from the kingdom of hostility into God's peace-loving kingdom. As they are the children of peace they can make peace with other nations and can call for the world to be reconciled to God and to each other (Colossians 1:20; 2 Corinthians 5:17-21).

3. The church is rooted and established in the love of Christ and therefore derives its name from the Holy God (Ephesians 3:15, 17). It has tasted God's righteousness and kissed His peace (Psalm 85:10). The followers of Christ, unlike all other philosophical and religious groups, are not established in human strength. They are, instead, established in the holiness of God whose love is absolute and unconditional.

For these reasons, the Bible calls the followers of Christ the salt and light of God for the world (Matthew 5:13-14); the salt that cleanses hearts from false values, beliefs and behaviors in order to preserve a good and righteous relationship with others; and the light that unveils the destructing values of ungodly beliefs in order to lead hearts and minds to the source of absolute love, justice and holiness.

Isn't it beautiful to be clothed with these characteristics? The key is "understanding". The knowledge of God produces a sincere heart with full assurance that leads people to the Light and to a life of peace with one another.

Bibliography and Resources for Further Study

Christian Worldview

Beckwith, Francis J., and Gregory Koukl, *Relativism: Feet Firmly Planted in Mid-Air*, Grand Rapid, MI: Baker Books, 1998.

Buswell, James Oliver Jr., *Christian View of Being and Knowing*, Grand Rapids, MI: Zondervan 1960.

Constance, Arthur C., *Man in Adam and in Christ*, Grand Rapids, MI: Zondervan, 1975.

Davies, Paul, *Superforce*, New York: Simon and Schuster, 1984.

Denton, Michael, *Evolution: A Theory in Crisis*, Bethesda MD: Adler and Adler, 1986.

Eidsmoe, John, *God and Caesar*, Westchester, IL: Crossway Books, 1985.

Erickson, Millard J., *Christian Theology* (Three Volumes), Grand Rapids, MI: Baker Book House, 1983.

Gilkey, London, *Maker of Heaven and Earth*, Garden City, NY: Doubleday 1959.

Henry, Carl F. H., *Christian Personal Ethics*, Grand Rapids, MI: Eerdmans, 1957.

Henry, Carl F. H., *God, Revelation and Authority* (Six Volumes), Waco, TX: Word Books, 1976.

Henry, Carl F. H., *Toward a Recovery of Christian Belief*, Westchester, IL: Crossway Books, 1990.

Henry, Carl F. H., *Twilight of a Great Civilization*, Westchester, IL: Crossway Books, 1988.

Horowitz, David, *Radical Son: A Generational Odyssey*, New York: The Free Press, 1997.

Jaki, Stanley L., *The Road of Science and the Ways to God*, Chicago: The University of Chicago Press, 1980.

Joad, C. E. M., *The Recovery of Belief*, London: Faber and Faber, 1955.

Kimball, Roger, *Tenured Radicals*, New York: Harper and Row, 1990.

Koestler, Arthur, and J. R. Smythies, eds., *Beyond Reductionism*, New York: Macmillan, 1970.

LaHaye, Tim, and David Noebel, *Mind Siege: The Battle for Truth in the New Millennium*, Nashville, TN: Word Publishers, 2001.

Lewis, C. S., *God in the Dock*, Grand Rapids, MI: Eerdmans, 1972.

Lovtrup, Soren, *Darwinism: The Refutation of a Myth*, London: Croom Helm, 1987.

Michaelsen, Jonathan, *Like Lam to the Slaughter*, Eugene, OR: Harvest House, 1989.

Montgomery, John Warwick, *Human Rights and Human Dignity*, Dallas, TX: Probe Books, 1986.

Montgomery, John Warwick, *The Law Above the Law*, Minneapolis: Dimension Books, 1975.

Noebel, David A., *The Battle For Truth*, Eugene, Oregon: Harvest House Publishing, 2001.

Roche, George C., *A World Without Heroes*, Hillsdale, MI: Hillsdale College Press, 1987.

Schaeffer, Francis A., *A Christian Manifesto*, Westchester, IL: Crossway Books, 1981.

Schaeffer, Francis A., *How Should We Then Live?*, Old Tappan, NJ: Fleming H. Revell, 1976.

Smith, A. E. Wilder, *Man's Origin, Man's Destiny*, Weathon, IL: Harold Show, 1968.

Smith, A. E. Wilder, *The Creation of Life*, Costa Mesa, CA: TWFT Publishers, 1970.

Stanmeyer, William, *Clear and Present Danger*, Ann Arbor, MI: Servant Books, 1983.

Trueblood, D. Elton, *Philosophy of Religion*, Grand Rapids, MI: Baker Book House, 1957.

Wells, Jonathan, *Icons of Evolution: Science or Myth?*, Washington DC: Regnery Publishing, Inc., 2000.

Whitehead, John W., *The Second American Revolution*, Westchester, IL: Crossway Books, 1988.

The Bible, NKJV.

Communist Worldview

Cornforth, Maurice, *The Open Philosophy and the Open Society*, New York: International Publishers, 1968.

Engels, Frederick, *Dialectic of Nature*, New York: International Publishers, 1976.

Lenin, V. I., *Complete Collected Works*, (Forty Five Volumes) Moscow: Progress Publisher, 1978.

Lenin, V. I., *Materialism and Empirio-Criticism*, New York: International Publishers, 1927.

Marx, Karl, *Introduction to Capital*, London, 1889.

Wetter, Gustav A. *Dialectical Materialism*, Westport, CT: Greenwood Press, 1977.

Humanist Worldview

Angeles, Peter, ed., *Critiques of God*, Buffalo: Prometheus Books, 1976.

Brockman, Chris, *What About God?*, Buffalo: Prometheus Books, 1978.

Dewey, John, *A Common Faith*, New Haven, CT: Yale University Press, 1934.

Egner, Robert E., and Lester E. Denon, eds., *The Basic Writings of Bertrand Russell*, New York: Simon and Schuster, 1961.

Ferguson, Marilyn, *The Aquarian Conspiracy*, Los Angeles: J. P. Tarcher, Inc., 1980.

Fromm, Erich, *You Shall Be as God*, New York: Holt, Rinehart and Winston, 1966.

Huxley, Julian, *Evolution: The Modern Synthesis*, New York: Harper and Brothers Publishers, 1942.

Huxley, Julian, *Religion Without Relativism*, New York: Mentor 1957.

Kurtz, Paul, ed., *Humanist Manifesto I and II*, Buffalo: Prometheus, 1980.

Kurtz, Paul, ed., *The Humanist Alternative*, Buffalo: Prometheus, 1973.

Lamont, Corliss, *The Illusion of Immortality*, New York: Frederick Ungar, 1965.

Lamont, Corliss, *The Philosophy of Humanism*, New York: Frederick Ungar Publishing, 1982.

Lamont, Corliss, *Voice in the Wilderness*, Buffalo: Prometheus, 1975.

Maslow, Abraham, *Toward a Psychology of Being*, New York: Van Nostrand Reinhold, 1968.

Potter, Charles F., "Humanism: A New Religion," 1930

Sagan, Carl, *Cosmos*, New York: Random House, 1980.

Sagan, Carl, *The Dragon of Eden*, New York: Random House, 1977.

Sellars, Roy Wood, *Evolutionary Naturalism*, Chicago: Open Court, 1922.

Stenger, Victor J., *Not By Design*, Buffalo Prometheus, 1988.

New Age

Adler, Vera, *When Humanity Comes of Age*, New York: Samuel Weiser, Inc., 1974.

Baer, Randall N., *Inside the New Age Nightmare*, Lafayette, LA: Huntington House, Inc., 1989.

Boritzer, Etan, *What Is God?*, Willowdale, On, Canada: Firely Books Ltd., 1990.

Campbell, Joseph, *The Power of Myth*, New York: Doubleday, 1988.

de Chardin, Pierre Teilhard, *The Phenomenon of Man*, New York: Harper and Row, 1955.

Gawain, Shakti, *Living in the Light, San Rafael*, CA: New World Library, 1986.

Halverson, Dean C., *Crystal Clear: Understanding and Reaching New Agers*, Colorado Springs, CO: NavPress, 1990.

Mueller, Robert, *The New Genesis: Shaping a Global Spirituality*, New York: Image Books, 1984.

Montgomery, Ruth, *A World Beyond*, New York: Ballantine/ Fawcett Crest Books, 1972.

Rowe, Ed, *The Age Globalization*, Herndon, Virginia: Growth Publishing, 1985.

Ryerson, Kevin, *Spirit Communication: The Soul's Path*, New York: Bantam Books, 1989.

Spangler, David, *Reflection On the Christ*, Scotland: Findhorn Publications, 1982.

Spangler, David, *Emergence: The Rebirth of the Sacred*, New York: Delta/Merloyd Lawrence, 1984.

Religious Worldviews

Anderson, J. N. D. (Editor), *The World's Religions,* London: Inter-Varsity Fellowship, 1951.

Cavendish, Richard, *The Great Religions*, London: Contact, 1980.

Eberhard, Wolfram, *A History of China,* London: Routledge & Kegan Paul Ltd. Pub., 1967.

Fairbank, John K. and Goldman, Merle, *China: A New History,* USA: The Belknap Press of Harvard University Press, 1998.

Halverson, Dean C. (General Editor), *World Religions,* Minneapolis, Minnesota: Bethany House Pub., 1996.

Heydt, Henry J., *A Comparison of World Religions*, USA: CLC, 1976.

Hunt, Arnold D. *Christ and the World's Religions,* Adelaide: The Griffin Press, 1970.

Langley, Myrtle, *Religions*, England: Lion Pub., 1981.

Lochhaas, Philip H., *The Eastern Religions,* USA, Missouri: Concordia Pub., 1970.

Mass, Nuri, *Many Paths One Heaven,* Australia, NSW: The Writers' Press, 1965.

Muhsin Khan, M. *Sahih Bukhari.* 9 vols. Published by Islamic University, Al Medina Al Munauwara, p.54, ND.)

Savage, Katharine, *The History of World Religions*, London: The Bodley Head, 1970.

Schirokauer, Conrad, *A Brief History of Chinese and Japanese Civilizations,* USA: Harcourt Brace Jovanovich, Inc., 1978.

Schlink, M. Basilea, *Christians and TM Yoga?,* Australia: Evangelical Sisterhood of Mary, 1975.

Sherratt, B. W. and Hawkin, D. J., *Gods and Men*, London: Blackie, 1972.

Siddiqi, Abdul Hamid, trans. 2000. *Sahih Muslim.* Rev. ed. 4 vols. New Delhi: Kitab Bhavan.

Stewart, Dicks & Mennil, Paul & Santor, Donald, *The Many Faces of Religion,* Canada: Ginn and Company, 1973.

Yamamoto, J. Isamu, *Buddhism, Taoism & Other Far Eastern Religions,* Michigan: Zondervan Pub., 1998.

Yamamoto, J. Isamu, *Hinduism, TM &Hare Krishna*, Michigan: Zondervan Pub., 1998.

'Comparing Christianity and Hinduism,' <http://www.catholiceducation.org/articles/apologetics/ap0008.html>.

'Endo and Johnston talk of Buddhism and Christianity,' (Interview with Novelist Shusaku Endo, Jesuit theologian William Johnston), <http://sino-sv3.sino.uni-heidelberg.de/FULLTEXT/JR-EPT/william1.htm>.

'The Divine Incarnation in Hinduism and Christianity,' <http://www.comparativereligion.com/avatars.html>.

'The Problem of Evil in World Religions,' 2002, <http://www.comparativereligion.com/evil.html>.

'The Ultimate Reality in World Religions,' 2002, <http://www.comparativereligion.com/man.html>.

The Koran.

The Avesta.

CPSIA information can be obtained at www.ICGtesting.com
Printed in the USA
BVOW04s1605160415

396398BV00001B/1/P

9 780975 601723